DAPHNE JONES

BULLETS AND BANDSMEN

**The story of a bandsman on the Western Front
written by his daughter**

First published September 1992

Published by OWL PRESS, PO BOX 315, Downton, Salisbury, Wiltshire. SP5 3YE
Printed and bound in Great Britain by SALISBURY PRINTING COMPANY LTD, Salisbury, Wiltshire.
Cover Design by Andrea Lee   Origination by OWL PRESS

British Library Cataloguing - in - Publication Data. A catalogue record for this book is available from the British Library.
ISBN 0 9515917 3 8

Acknowledgements

Thanks for help to the following:
(The late) Mrs Dawn Button, TocH, Chippenham
Major (Retd) R.D.W. McLean and the staff of the Museum of the Staffordshire Regiment
The Mayor of Noeux-les-Mines, Pas de Calais
MOD Departmental Record Office
Mr Anthony Pates
Public Records Office, Kew
TocH Wendover
The Trustees of the Imperial War Museum
Mr and Mrs G. P. Whitehouse, Brocton
(and the family for putting up with mess....)

Contents

France 1917

France 1918

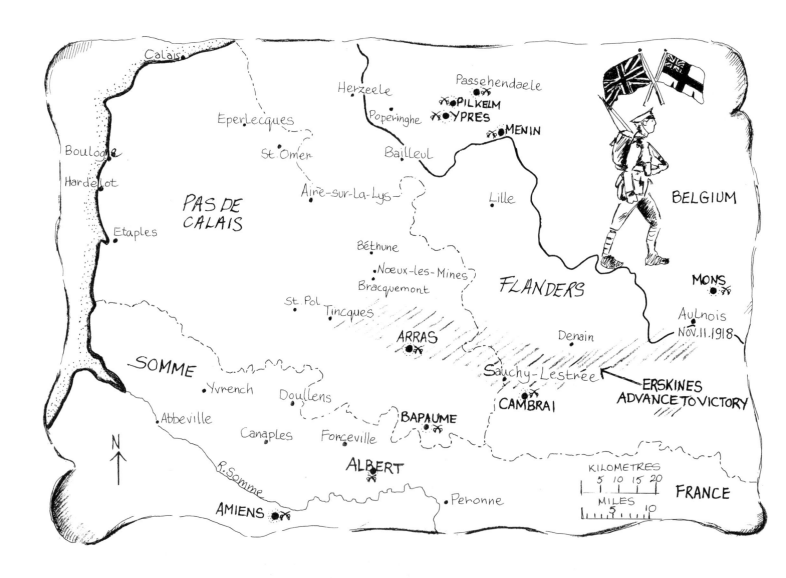

Introduction

ERSKINE Williams was an artist, a musician and, for three unforgettable years during the Great War, a soldier. Born in South London in 1881 during the reign of Queen Victoria, he was already well into his thirties when the war began in the summer of 1914.

His letters from the Front entertained the postman too

Bullets and Bandsmen

The following year under the Derby Scheme, he 'attested his willingness to enlist' and opted for service as an Army bandsman. In March 1916 he reported for training at Brocton Camp in Staffordshire and at the end of the year sailed for France where he served until the war was over.

Throughout his time in the Army Erskine drew vivid, off-the-cuff pen and ink sketches of the people he met and the places he visited, sending them home to Tooting where his father, Edward Williams, pasted them into a book. It is these drawings, with extracts from letters and the diary he kept while serving in France, which form the basis for this book. It tells in fascinating detail the everyday story of life behind the Lines in the Great War.

Wherever the 11th Division went the Divisional Band went too, from one battle zone to the next. For the bandsmen there were all kinds of contrasts. Though their main task was to cheer up the wounded and weary men snatching a few hours leave from the Line, they had other less pleasant jobs to do as well. One day they could be entertaining officers in a château, the next they might be burying the dead, men or horses, from the latest push along the Front. Another time they would be playing for a concert party, the shells screaming overhead, just hours after guarding German prisoners of war.

Erskine was 35, practically middle-aged, by the time he began his basic training. At Brocton Camp he was surrounded mainly by young men in their teens and twenties from every walk of life. He was by nature a quiet, thoughtful and intelligent man and he made acute observations of the life around him. He noted in extraordinary depth many unrecorded aspects of the war, bringing to life the humdrum day-to-day events as he saw them. Whether it was learning how to load a rifle or lining up for a vaccination before leaving for France, he noted it all in graphic detail.

His training in observation began at a young age. He was born with artistic talents and as a small boy of eight, Erskine had toured the music halls with his father drawing likenesses, at incredible speed, of famous people of the day. Because of his size he had to stand on a box to reach the easel. He sketched from memory while an orchestra played softly in the background. For his act he wore a velvet suit with a big lace collar and on his small chest two rows of medals which had been presented to him by admirers of his talent. He drew Queen Victoria, Gladstone and many famous people of the day; as the face took shape the audience would recognise who it was and break into loud applause. The pair of them travelled all over the United Kingdom and the Continent and performed in Australia, New Zealand and the USA.

When Erskine was a young man he went to work as a technical illustrator for a weekly magazine called *The Chauffeur and Garage Gazette* (price one penny) that had its offices in Long Acre in London. He was fascinated by motor vehicles and drew all the early motor cars - such as the Talbot, the Delage, the Spyker and the Cadillac - as well as their working parts. Understandably this journal ceased publication shortly after the war began - motoring was becoming a luxury and the chauffeurs were going into the services. Until he joined up he worked with his father in the family signwriting business.

Erskine dressed for the stage

Erskine had always been musical, playing the violin and the clarinet when he was a boy. However, his great love was the oboe and it was because he had one of his own that he found himself in France in December 1916 ready to join the band of the 11th Division of the British Expeditionary Force (BEF).

The two years he spent in France and Belgium were quite unlike the experience of tens of thousands of infantrymen, who were sent to the Front as soon as they landed at Boulogne. He was often on the move and travelled hundreds of miles - on foot, by train, in the back of a lorry and even by London bus.

Although he had performed in front of huge audiences as a young boy and had spent much of his childhood in the company of adults, he was a shy man. He was not one for drinking, though smoking was another matter, and he rarely swore or even raised his voice. Life in the Army brought many surprises.

Erskine and his treasured oboe

Training at Brocton Camp

WHEN Erskine reported to Brocton Camp in the spring of 1916 he was just one among thousands of raw recruits who had been sent there to be turned into soldiers. The camp, built hurriedly on windswept Cannock Chase, consisted of row after row of long wooden huts; the 'Lines'. There were two camps on the site: Brocton, south-east of Stafford, with its huge steel water tank, visible from every direction, and Rugeley Camp, which owed its name to the nearby town.

On 5 March 1916 John Guy, bandmaster to the 13th (Reserve) Battalion, of the Nottinghamshire and Derbyshire Regiment - otherwise known as The Sherwood Foresters - had written to Erskine at his home.

> Dear Sir,
> As you are engaged for this band, kindly report yourself to join the nearest recruiting office and ask to be sent to this battalion when you will be given a warrant. Ask the officer to send you direct to this camp - let me know per return.
> Yours truly,
>
> *John Guy*

The letter was addressed to Mr E.Williams (oboe) and across the corner were written the words 'own instrument'. Erskine duly replied. Exactly one week later he said goodbye to his father and four sisters and made his way to the recruiting office at Kingston, in Surrey, where he was given his travel warrant to Brocton Camp.

Bullets and Bandsmen

Erskine had originally volunteered for a Short Service Engagement on 16 November 1915, two months before compulsory conscription was finally introduced by the Government by Lord Derby, Secretary for War from 1916-1918. This was the 'Derby' scheme, whereby men of military age 'attested' - that is to say they agreed to serve when they were needed. Two and a half million men answered this particular call to arms.

Men who attested were given the option of choosing the occupation they would follow when they finally joined up. Erskine opted to be a bandsman. It was probably as well that he had volunteered because if he had not, as an able-bodied unmarried man, he was liable to be accosted in the street by a woman, handed a white feather and asked why he was not in uniform.

Erskine was a member of 'D' Company of the Sherwood Foresters. He was duly kitted out in khaki and a dab hand at managing the puttees that he wound around his lower leg. However he had yet to make contact with many other musicians - there were none in the hut where he was living at first. He wrote home,

> Dear Pa and Emily,
>   Pleased to report some improvement in the state of affairs. The new arrival (another bandsman) is a go ahead personage and has dug out two other musicians and introduced me to them - one a good young clarinettist and flautist who will make a decent pal I think.
>   I spent the morning in what they call the Band Hut and we had a sort of informal rehearsal. The bandmaster hasn't returned yet from his quest of other bandsmen but it's supposed he will return with about 15 of them, so the report runs. I hope he does so we can make a start.
>   I've borrowed this (writing) paper from a very youthful soldier, just like a long kid. He's only 15 - doesn't seem possible - and has twice been in the draft for the Front and been taken out of it owing to his youth. He can do all the

soldiers' work and carry the 96lbs of equipment. Doesn't appear credible.

This morning had sausage (in the singular) for breakfast, slightly burnt on the side in contact with pan. The remarks of the men on the subject were most illuminating. The officers pop in and ask 'Any complaints' and receive the stentorian stereotyped answer of 'No, Sir'.

Brocton Camp was like a self-contained town; it had its own post office and even a branch of W H Smith, where Erskine bought a packet of postcards on which to draw his sketches. There was a canteen run by the Navy and Army Canteen Board (a sort of early NAAFI) and a YMCA hut, too, with billiard tables and reading rooms. There was even a camp railway linking up with Milford station on the main line.

Schools of instruction were dotted all over the site and a few weeks after Erskine arrived he began his training. On 7 April he sent home to 158 High Street, Tooting, first of many illustrated postcards. He wrote,

'This is what we are doing now. They are beautiful little rifles to handle.'

Bandsmen in all shapes and sizes

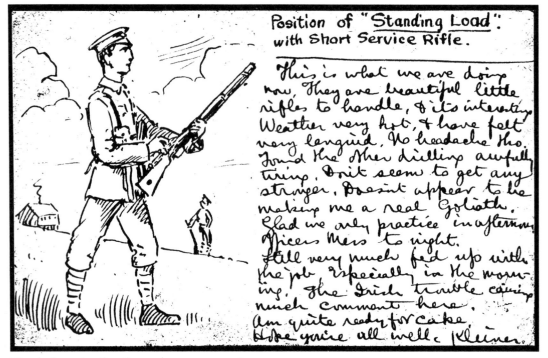

Training took place every morning

Throughout his life he had suffered severe headaches; they were to be a recurring theme in his correspondence throughout the next three years. The weather was warm for early April and he found the training both exhausting and liable to bring them on. He told his father,

'Don't seem to be getting any stronger, doesn't appear to be making me a real Goliath'.

He added that he and the other bandsmen were beginning to practise together now in the afternoons and that night were to be play in the Officers' Mess. He ended his message: 'Am quite ready for cake'. (Showing his enthusiasm for a food parcel from home.)

Erskine on bayonet practice

Bullets and Bandsmen

Previously Erskine had always played his instruments, whether it was the oboe, the violin or the clarinet, sitting comfortably on a chair in a concert hall with a music stand in front of him. Although there would be plenty of occasions when he performed that way in the Army he now had to learn to play as he marched along. He wrote,

> 'Getting on well with the little clarinet on the march. Rather hard work though; think the larger clarinet would be better. Marched about seven miles, nice and slow, feet more comfy.' (Heavy Army boots took some getting used to.)

After the rifle drill sessions came bayonet training - and another sketch.

> 'Your little son at it. This is a thrust at the heart of an imaginary Deutscher. There are rows of these white patches representing vital parts. It's rare sport but hard work. The sack on the floor is another German. Route march today at slower pace. No ill effects at all'.

From his early years Erskine's family nickname had been 'Kleiner' - meaning 'little' in German - and that is how he signed many of the postcards. In view of the 'hate the Hun' campaign that was sweeping the country, fuelled by newspaper stories of alleged atrocities, this was probably rather unwise. Fortunately nobody seemed to have noticed.

The training was relentless and quite unlike anything he - or many of the other bandsmen - had done before. He explained his latest energetic exercise to his father,

> 'Jumping into trench - part of last day at Range. It's a series of advances from 600 yards; keep advancing then lying flat and firing. Up again and forward

Erskine practises the advance

get in trench, fire over parapet, on again, etc.

The rifle looks too short, but this is quite right. This firing is done with a row of men, not singly as shown. Rifle loaded with real 'uns.'

Then there was bomb throwing practice,

'This is a charming pastime we indulged in, in the rain, for three hours. Hope this is a clear illustration, especially of the rain.

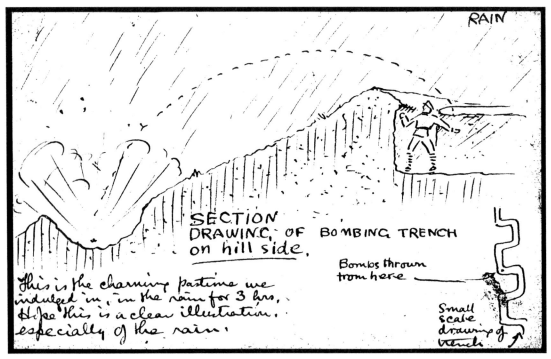

Throwing grenades in the rain

How we instruct at squad drill (another good subject for a sketch) This is how we do it. Have to stand away from the squad and shout it out, very big, like this. It's not as easy as it looks but I'm not the worst. Cheek is what you want all the time, not ability.' (He added: 'The cake arrived.')

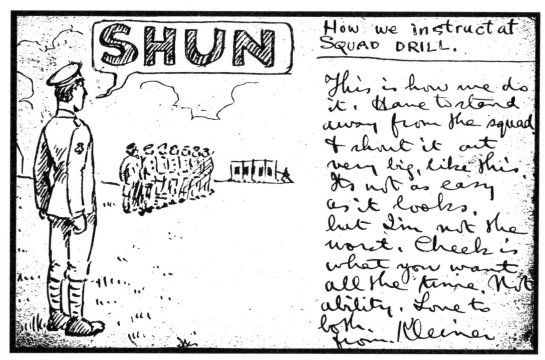

Taking his turn at drilling the squad

As well as training in the arts of war and playing with the band there were tasks of a domestic nature to be carried out as well, such as 'peeling taters'. This time he used one of the special YMCA postcards which carried the stirring message 'For God, For King and For Country'.

'This takes place before breakfast. I generally do some. Observe cascade of peelings. Very hot at this. Still not allowed out of camp.'

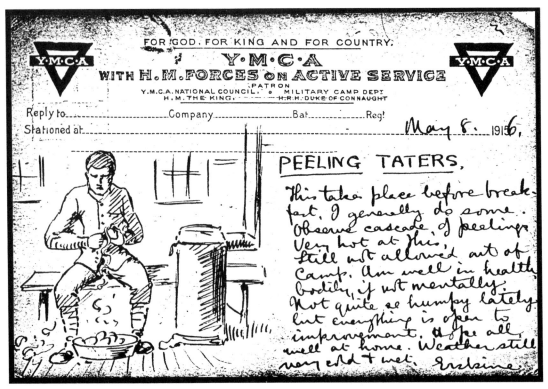

A dab hand at peeling potatoes

However this situation would change very shortly and the news that some leave was on the way was greeted with joy. It would be good to get home, even if only for a short weekend. In early May, a few days before he went on leave Erskine, along with many others, lined up to be vaccinated, against what he did not say. He wrote home,

'This ordeal came off on Wednesday morning. We were all very brave (I don't

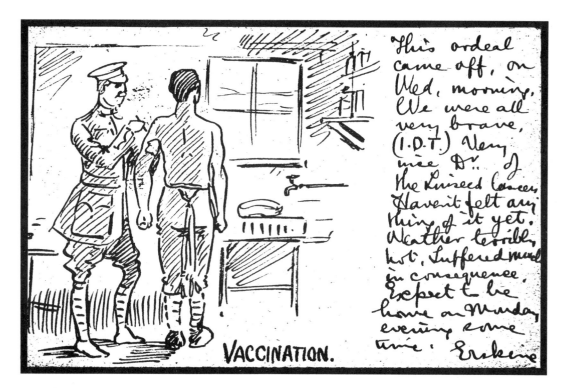

A brave face for the doctor

think). Very nice doctor of the Linseed Lancers (the Medical Corps). Haven't
felt anything of it yet. Expect to be home on Monday evening some time.'

Erskine and his pals

Naturally his father and those of his sisters who were not away in service, were delighted to see him when he arrived in London a few days later and eager to hear what he had been doing. The short leave went only too quickly and in no time at all he was on the train back to Brocton.

It was about this time that Erskine and two of his musician friends posed for a picture to send home to their families, their instruments in their hands - Commander with his clarinet, 'Cockney' with his cornet and he with his oboe.

The bus called Daisy

By now the band of the Sherwood Foresters was going out on playing jobs, travelling by charabanc or bus. This was an ideal subject for one of his more humorous cards.

Over in France the bloody Battle of the Somme was about to begin and the men, their training complete, are leaving in great numbers for the Front. Whenever the troops left Brocton to set off for the Front they were given a musical farewell, even if it happened to be in the middle of the night.

A musical send off

'Departure of draft for the Front at 1a.m. Wednesday. Played off by band on platform. Great enthusiasm. Very stirring sight. Band playing Auld Lang Syne as train leaves station. Got to camp at about 3 a.m. tired.'

Embarkation Approaches

MAIL from home and the next meal, both announced by a call on the bugle, were the most important events of the day. 'Letters from Lousy Lucy' was a reminder of home (would there be one for me today ?) but 'Come to the Cookhouse Door' was almost as eagerly awaited.

The morning bugle call

Food was a constant topic of conversation and featured in a number of Erskine's sketches. On one occasion he drew his father a picture of an average breakfast,

'Thought sketch of grub might be interesting. It's very important here I might add.'

An average breakfast

Sometimes it was his turn to fetch the early morning tea,(or 'gunfire', a military term from a century earlier).

'I only fetch the tea occasionally....when you get there it's generally all gone.'

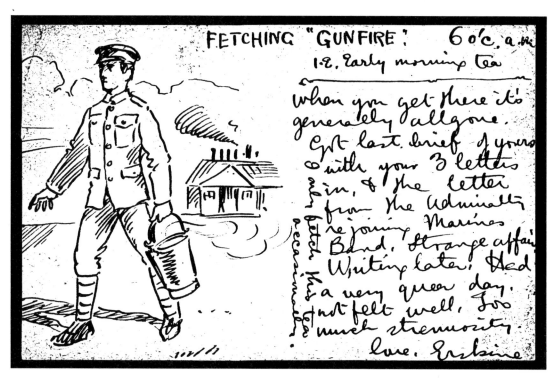

Fetching 'gunfire'

Sometimes he helped the Orderly Man fetch the breakfast from the cookhouse.

'We should be wearing hats, except the Sergeant Cook......we are still doing our musketry every morning.'

Helping in the cookhouse

The last hot meal of their day was at 4.30 p.m. in the afternoon so it was not surprising that by evening time everyone was hungry again. This usually meant a visit to the canteen or to a nearby pub or maybe just sharing out a food parcel from home. One day in August the band were set the task of washing the floor of their hut.

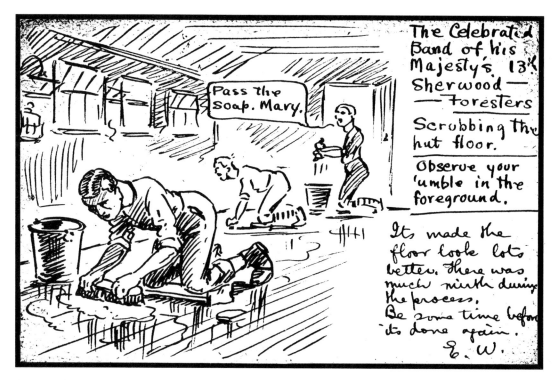

Pass the soap Mary

'The celebrated band of His Majesty's 13th Sherwood Foresters scrubbing the hut floor - observe your 'umble in the foreground. It's made the floor lots better. Be some time before it's done again.'

He noted on the card that there was much mirth during the process.

A less strenuous and much more satisfying chore that Erskine was given to do was repairing the band parts. His postcard home gave a hint of the Foresters' repertoire; overtures were always popular - pieces like 'William Tell', 'Poet and Peasant' and 'The Thief of Baghdad'. He noted

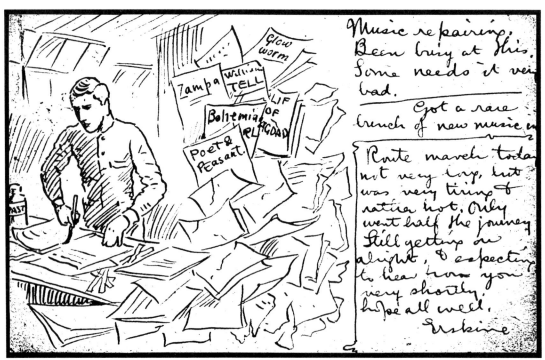

Repairing music

that they had got a 'rare bunch of new music in'.

In September his artistic talents came in useful when some handbills were needed to advertise a Sunday concert by the band of the 12th Battalion Training Reserve (late 13th Sherwood Foresters), as they were now designated. Always resourceful, he used one of his bed trestles to help him steady his hand as he carefully painted the lettering. He wrote on this card,

'The cake, etc, just received...pineapple a treat. We had it between about 6 of us, with sardines.'

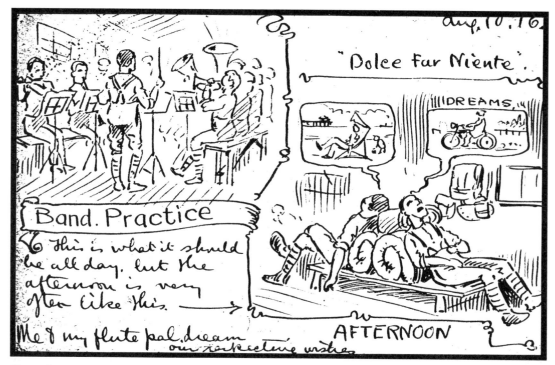

Band practice

Band practice was supposed to take up most of the time once their training sessions were over but the afternoons were often spent 'having a kip', dreaming about what they would like to be doing if they were not otherwise engaged.

Though they did not rehearse quite as much as they were supposed to they often went out on playing jobs. On one occasion, at Longton Park, they lined up for a photograph. Erskine sent a copy home to his sister Emily. He wrote,

The Foresters' band

'Thought you would like a photo of our band taken at a Sunday performance at Longton Park, Staffs. I look a rough customer with the oboe don't I ? Can you find any nice boys in this band?'

The Foresters' Band had the use of a Northern Counties bus and once, after they had been playing in Walsall, it broke down, with a damaged rear axle. There was nothing for it but to get out and walk, arriving back at camp at half-past three in the morning. It didn't seem so funny at the time but it made a good subject for a sketch.

Walking back to camp in the early hours

During another spell of leave Erskine visited his brother Frank in Cannock, which was a short bus ride from the camp. Fortunately this was before the town was temporarily put out of bounds following some 'unfortunate incidents' concerning alcohol. Not surprisingly the local traders were appalled at this decision because they had been doing nicely out of the influx of so many potential customers and so the order was rescinded. After spending a while with his brother Frank, Erskine took the train to Birmingham to visit his older brother Charley who owned a cinema, The Scala, in the centre of the town - a cue for another drawing. He wrote,

> 'Charley and I taking tea in the palatial lounge. The lady attendant kindly did the amiable.'

The lounge at the Scala

This leisurely and civilised scene was in sharp contrast to the situation back at Brocton, where there was 'drill all the time'.

Throughout the autumn, as well as rehearsing and performing, Erskine continued his training; erecting barbed wire entanglements formed the basis for a card.

Barbed wire entanglements

'A job after your own heart,' he told his father. 'Observe the corkscrew iron uprights. Great idea. Men follow on with coils of wire and place (it) through the eye holes. Very smart. I've had a go at it. This is a noiseless method instead of driving wood posts in. Always has to be done at night.'

Gas mask drill was an aspect of training that he certainly did not enjoy; practising marching while playing their instruments, though tiring, was much more enjoyable. On one occasion, when they were out in the countryside, they were ordered to stop for a rest and as the hedges were thick with blackberries they took the opportunity to eat as many as they could.

Blackberry picking at a halt on the march

Meanwhile the 11th (Northern) Division of the British Expeditionary Force was fighting on the Somme. It had been formed in August 1914, the month when the war began, in Grantham, Lincolnshire, and at first consisted entirely of north country battalions including the Sherwood Foresters and the South Staffs, though men of the Dorsets joined it later. By September the combined strength of the infantry was 13,000 men.

On 30 June the following year the Division embarked from Liverpool on two troopships, the Aquitania and the Empress of Britain, and by August men were fighting in the Dardanelles. They were at the landing at Suvla - and at the evacuation the following December.

In January 1916 the Division left for Egypt where they stayed until June, when instructions were received to embark for France. By the end of July the 11th Division had taken over part of VI Corps front line (in the Third Army) and in September were fighting on the Somme near Albert, in the Battles of Flers-Courcelette (15-22 September) and Thiepval Ridge (26-28 September).

A few weeks before Christmas, Erskine completed his training and was advised to apply to join the Division's band. He was given the name of the bandmaster, Mr K A White, and the address to write to; by now the DHQ was at Forceville, not many miles from where the battles had been fought the previous September.

The reply came back almost immediately; it was dated 5 December,

'In reply to your letter wishing to join my band I should be very pleased to have you as an oboe player. I am sorry to say I am quite helpless to do anything further in the matter till you actually land in France. When you do land write to me at once giving your full address. I shall then do my best to get you into the band. I should like you to bring your oboe with you as we do not have one out here. Should I be successful in getting you into the band you will find it a very nice occupation.'

Off to the Western Front

WHEN it was Erskine's turn to leave Brocton for the Western Front there was no band playing on the railway platform because he was setting out on his own. He took the train to Euston and found it still awash with service people, as it had been when he had travelled south to see his father back in the summer. After stopping for a cup of tea he made his way across London to Victoria where he caught the train to Folkestone. He would have liked to have called in at Tooting to see his father while he was in London but there just was not time.

The day before, 10 December, he had been transferred from the Sherwood Foresters to the South Staffs Regiment and now he was on the way to France to join the 11th (Northern) Division of the British Expeditionary Force and become a member of its band.

He had no idea what lay before him; the news of the fighting on the Somme that summer had been reported in the British newspapers but to the readers it seemed a long, long way away; the wounded returning home and those men lucky enough to get leave were curiously silent about the carnage they had witnessed.

General Haig's offensive had begun on the first day of July; thirteen British divisions had gone 'over the top' and in no time at all 19,000 men lay dead and another 57,000 were wounded. The bloody Battle of the Somme had gone on for months, petering out just a few weeks earlier.

Erskine had been to the Continent a number of times before when he was a small boy appearing on the music halls, but that seemed a century ago. The ferry ride from Folkestone across the English Channel to Boulogne was uneventful, the heavily-laden ship taking care to keep to the prescribed L-shaped route that was alleged to be free from bobbing mines and marauding U-boats. Boulogne was where practically every serviceman - and woman - first set foot in France , while Calais, along the coast, was the main port of entry for supplies.

Over the top , Battle of the Somme

When he disembarked Erskine reported to the Depot Battalion and was told where he would be spending the weeks until he joined the Division. The next day he took the train to Albert, a large town on the Somme which bore the unmistakable signs of bombing. It was about 28 kilometres north-east of Amiens, cathedral city and regional capital, which was to suffer its own devastation in August 1918. From Albert he managed to get a lift as far as Englebelmer, once a village full of country folk and farm animals but now just a jumble of ruined cottages and barns, a sight that Erskine would come across over and over again in his travels in the next two years.

Forceville, the Division and - hopefully - a hot meal were still five kilometres away; there was no form of transport available so there was nothing for it but to march there, on his own, in the pouring rain. His full kit, covered by his waterproof cape and containing his precious oboe, was heavy on his back, and walking was difficult; the road, such as it was, consisted of uneven logs, laid in the mud to provide some sort of surface for vehicles - and for tired and weary bandsmen.

When he finally arrived at Forceville, the headquarters of the Support Brigade, he managed to locate No 25 Billet and report to the bandmaster. The band itself was just off to entertain one of the infantry battalions but he would be able to meet them later on. By this time he was starving hungry and as soon as he found the band's billet he located the cook - 'a taciturn man' - who gave him the long-awaited hot dinner.

Throughout its travels the 11th Divisional Headquarters (DHQ) kept an official the War Diary (now kept in the Public Records Office in Kew). For most of the time, wherever the DHQ went, the band - and Erskine - went, too. On 4 January 1917, Erskine arrived in Forceville. The War Diary notes, 'Artillery active both by day and night. Enemy artillery active during the morning.' Erskine wrote in his new diary that night,

> 'I got chummy with some chaps belonging to the Divisional concert party....the accommodation for billeting here is very rough - dark barn, wire netting beds,

over run with rats at night....was glad to get into band, start the New Year under strange conditions.'

The next few weeks were hectic, what with getting to know the other members of the band, who came from all walks of life and from various regiments, and practising his music. Breakfast was at 8 a.m. each morning, cooked by one of the bandsmen, and daily practice took place between 10 a.m. and noon in a tumbledown shed that doubled as the Divisional cinema. Erskine shared a music stand with the third clarinet player.

'We have oboe parts for all selections but deficient for a lot of marches and brass band stuff. Find I'm not in a very good playing form.'

Erskine's first billet in France

A CORNER OF OUR BILLET. FORCEVILLE

SOMME

Bullets and Bandsmen

This was because for the last few months back in England with the Foresters' band, Erskine had played E flat clarinet, a stubby, shorter clarinet, which had set him back with the oboe. However the Bandmaster was lenient and passed no caustic comments for which he was grateful. 'My reeds are rather defective,' he noted.

Now that he was further from home, letters (and the occasional parcel) were even more eagerly awaited. One of the first to arrive when he got to Forceville was from his niece Maggie. She had drawn a series of pictures including some pigs and wrote in careful childish handwriting,

A few little pigs

'Dear Uncle Erskine,
 I am just writing you a little letter to show you how I have coppied (sic) these pigs and I wish you a happy New Year. I would like you to write me a long letter back.'

One of the parcels that had caught up with him contained a Christmas pudding but instead of eating it all in one go Erskine and his pals had made the mistake of leaving some of it overnight - to the delight of the rats. He wrote in his diary,

'These rodents are very annoying after lights out...hear them scuttling about playing old Harry.'

No sooner was he getting used to life at Forceville than orders came that they were to move, the first of many such upheavals that would take them hundreds of miles around the French countryside over the next two years.

Off on an outside job

On 18 January the band packed up their kit and most of them marched off, leaving Erskine and three other musicians to follow on by lorry with the instruments. Before they could set off they had to clean out the billet and in the course of sweeping up discovered a quantity of food that had been left behind. On this occasion the rats had been thwarted, because it was all tinned.

The next few days were spent travelling west, in the opposite direction to the Line, stopping off at a different billet each night. Their destination, though they did not know it at the time, was to be Yvrench, a small town north-east of Abbeville, where the Division was to undergo a period of intensive training.

Erskine was familiar with most types of motor vehicle because of his work as a technical illustrator so he noted in his diary that the lorry they were travelling in was a Silent Knight Sleeve Valve Daimler. The roads were hard and pitted with holes and he wrote,

> 'Lorry bumped and rocked like a coastal steamer in heavy weather - still better than marching.'

Erskine and the other three men in the lorry met up with the rest of the band at Candas, 20 kilometres or so from Forceville, on the first night. There they unloaded the instruments, along with blankets, spare kit and general stores, and put up for the night in a bow hut. It had been pouring for days but the rain had stopped by now and a hard frost set in.

> 'Our little party (still) left in charge of luggage, not the faintest idea where we're going...awfully cold.'

Domquer was their next port of call where they stayed the night in 'a terrible apology of a lodging, a sort of stable'. There was no glass in the windows and no door in the doorway but they managed to make themselves comfortable on the straw-covered floor.

The next morning was fine, and after a shave and breakfast they cleared up and loaded the lorry, ready for a cold but interesting journey through St Riquier, another cathedral town. The roads all the way were frozen, bearing the impressions of hoof and footmarks, and they remained like that for over a month.

As frequently happened on their journeys, they managed to get lost once or twice but eventually the little party arrived at Yvrench, a long straggly village, where the billet turned out to be a large barn with a thatched roof. There were no windows and it was freezing cold; the three-tier beds were made of wire netting and Erskine settled for one in the middle. The bottom bunks were never used for sleeping purposes, only for storage.

> 'Never experienced such a time - only known the temperature lower and that was in New York.' (Where he had appeared on the stage in the winter of 1899-1900.) 'This night was the coldest I have passed. Chaps very busy improvising a brazier of fire. The trouble is to salvage wood to burn in it.'

The bitter cold was the all-absorbing topic of conversation; washing in the morning was an ordeal. To make matters worse, Erskine was a sensitive man and at first had been unhappy in the band. According to his diary he had received the 'cold shoulder' because 'new faces were not approved of.' This mainly arose because many of the other musicians were soldiers who had seen some action; Erskine had never fought in the trenches and therefore was not 'qualified'. He wrote in his diary,

> 'It's necessary to cultivate a good thick skin......may wear off in time.'

Fortunately the Bandmaster was easy to get on with and after a while he was accepted by the band as 'one of us', the early animosity forgotten. In time he made a number of pals and had already become friendly with another newcomer who had also joined the band at Forceville. This was Lance Corporal Stone of the West Yorks Regiment, a man in his forties and an accomplished clarinet player.

Bullets and Bandsmen

Before the month came to an end they had to move out of one cold, draughty, tumbledown barn into another at the opposite end of the village. Erskine was too late to get one of the wire beds so he made up his bedding on the floor along with Ginger Wood, the second cornet in the band. In the coming months he was to prove a very good pal indeed.

Playing outside in freezing weather was no pleasure; for one thing everybody's fingers were terribly cold and it affected the instruments, too. The valves on the brass instruments froze up and more than once Erskine's oboe keys stuck down with frost. Sometimes the audience was small to say the least, such as the time in Yvrench when a pig and a couple of chickens were the sum total.

Playing outside in the winter

Erskine wrote,

> 'Perceive the kind gent in middle distance with two dixies of tea for our refreshment.'

Occasionally the cold weather had its compensations. One day early in February they went some distance by lorry to play to the Royal Artillery near Auxi-le-Chateau. They had their instruments with them but the wagon containing the music and the stands was late arriving, so to while away the time the band amused themselves, like a bunch of schoolboys, by sliding up and down on a frozen brook ('great sport'). The wagon with the music never did turn up so they hitched a lift back to their billet.

Will the wagon ever turn up? 'San fairy Ann!'

From Billet to Billet

S ATURDAY 17 February was Erskine's 36th birthday ('no presents', he wrote in his diary) and to mark the occasion he drew in Indian ink, on the back of a letter to his father, a corner of his billet. He explained,

> 'The rolled up parcel on the floor is my bed, which I prefer on the floor to sleeping up on the top storey. It's warm on the floor. Today the brazier hasn't been in use....sufficiently warm to do without it. Observe my oboe, and tin hat and haversack which I use as cupboards'.

Band practice at Yvrench took place in a small room above the BEF canteen. Not only was it warm it was also handy for a cup of tea and a wedge of fruit cake when they had finished playing. Sometimes they gave a concert in the canteen where huge oil lamps provided the illumination. When an officer was present he was always given the place of honour in the front row.

A few days later they were off on their travels, marching in the rain to a village called Canaples on the road to Amiens. Erskine needed some new reeds for his oboe and when they came to a small town called Bernaville he was lucky enough to find a music shop and buy what he wanted. When they reached Canaples and found their billet, an empty house, they dried themselves out and shortly afterwards their instruments turned up on a lorry. They were only going to be there a few days, just long enough to play for the Royal Engineers and the East Yorks Regiment at Pernois, a few kilometres away.

On 23 February they packed up yet again, with the prospect of a much longer march. Their destination was Marieux, a town 15 kilometres south-east of the fortified city of Doullens. They were due to stay there until the spring. The War Diary notes the state of the roads, 'Moving a matter of great difficulty...roads almost impossible for transport.'

A corner of the billet

It was hard on the marchers, too, and Erskine got one of his headaches; he lacked the stamina of the younger men and his smoking did not help. Soon after he arrived he wrote a short note home,

> 'A line to let you know all's well. Am writing from a different place now. Am well. Had few spasms of neuralgia but it passes off. No parcels to hand since hearing from you last.'

Their new billet, definitely the best to date, was in some out buildings in the grounds of a fine old château which, as was often the case, had been commandeered as the DHQ. Instead of straw (and its problems with rats), the floor was made of smooth tiles for this was where the fruit from the orchard was usually dried.

Filling dixies from a well

The grounds of the château had been beautifully kept and although the trees were bare it was an ideal setting for the band to play for the headquarters staff. When they gave concerts indoors, in the Officers' Mess, candle lamps were attached to their stands so that they could see their music. They practised regularly in a barn near their billet - Erskine using his new music stand - and for the next five or six weeks, with just the occasional day off, they were out and about all over the area entertaining different service units. The Royal Flying Corps was always a favourite audience; for one thing the band was always given plenty to eat.

The aerodrome was situated on a level plateau near Marieux and the planes were a constant source of interest. Another popular venue was the Field Ambulance Brigade at Beauval, just south of Doullens. Here again they were right royally treated to 'a capital tea' followed by a break neck trip back to the billet - by motor ambulance.

The projection room of the Divisional Cinema

A little to the north of Marieux was village called Sarton where the Divisional cinema outfit was located. Erskine wrote home,

'This you can bet is a great source of interest to me.'

45

Compared to his brother's cinema in Birmingham it was primitive in the extreme but it gave immense enjoyment to the men who crowded into the 'picture palace'. The operator was a soldier called Firth who used a petrol engine and dynamo to provide the power.

There was a solemn occasion on 23 February when the band played the Dead March at the funeral of an officer who had been killed in action the week before. He wrote,

'I played cymbals...impressive...local fire brigade there in full rig.'

The officer's death was a poignant reminder that while they were comparatively safe behind the Lines. The infantrymen from their Division were fighting in the trenches.

There were many happier occasions when they played; at football matches and sports days and on one afternoon, for the South Staffs, Erskine's own Regiment. Another time, at Sarton, they played a few light pieces before a pierrot show began. This was not their own outfit, the 'Wunny Wuns', but the 'Shell Shifters', so called because they were attached to the ammunition column. He noted,

'It was a capital show - very high class.'

By now it was April and the United States had declared war on Germany. On Monday, 9 April, the Battle of Arras began and the following day the Canadians captured Vimy Ridge. The band had spent almost seven weeks at Marieux in their comfortable billet in the grounds of the château but on 11 April they packed up to leave because the Division was on the move again. Erskine helped load the lorry with their things and was lucky enough to get a lift while the other members of the band marched east along the Albert Road to Acheux, the next village to Forceville. They were almost back to square one.

This time they were billeted again close to the DHQ but their quarters were nowhere near as good. They would only be at Acheux for about a week and then they would be heading north.

The cookhouse at Marieux

Until the instruments (and the bandmaster) arrived, they spent most of their time on fatigues; some of the bandsmen cleaned the officers' cars and Erskine did some signwriting and painting jobs. The War Diary notes about this time that the Division had been placed under the Fifth Army and allotted to the Vth Corps.

While they were at Acheux the massive British onslaught on the German lines was taking place at Arras less than 30 kilometres to the north. Erskine made no mention of this in his diary although he must have been aware of it. The Battle of Arras 9-14 April, was won at the cost of 142,000 men, and the British casualties were said to out number the German by almost two to one - for a gain of three precious miles.

The British captured 11,000 prisoners of war and Erskine wrote,

> 'One evening we played outside the YM hut and while there we saw a huge batch of German prisoners pass to the cage. Spoke to some of them where they halted. They looked in every stage of exhaustion.....most pitiable objects.'

Tuesday, 17 April was hot and sticky and the band packed up and set off early, marching through Forceville, then through a number of tiny villages - Hedauville and Bouzincourt and the ruined village of Aveluy by-passing the town of Albert.

They marched passed Crucifix Corner and on to Ovillers. A night's rest brought welcome relief, sleeping in a hut on the site of a battlefield. The band was now in the area where, a year earlier, the famous Battle of the Somme had been fought by the men who answered Kitchener's call; hundreds of thousands of volunteers were mown down by the German machine guns. Today the map is peppered with symbols, showing the cemetries where they lie. The number of British troops who were killed, wounded or reported missing is estimated at 420,000.

Before they left Ovillers Erskine saw the grave of the son of Sir Harry Lauder. The famous Scottish music hall star was a household name at that time. 'Roamin' in the Gloamin', 'I Love a Lassie' and 'A Wee Doch and Doris', were three of the songs he used to sing and it was said he wrote 'Keep Right On to the End of the Road' after his son was killed. They left Ovillers and passed through more devastated villages, Pozières and Le Sars. Finally they stopped just outside the town of Bapaume on the Péronne Road. They pitched camp amongst the shell holes, half way between Beaulencourt and Riencourt, villages which were 'all heaps of bricks'.

Six of the tents were allocated to the band who now had to get down to some serious practice, as well as carrying out their more mundane duties. Erskine was appointed line orderly and had signwriting work to do as well. The bandmaster asked him to renovate the paintwork on the band's big drum and he wrote home,

Renovating the band's big drum

'I did it pretty decent with my one brush. In need of some Bright Red (*paint*). The BM is very anxious to have the coat of arms touched up a bit as it is somewhat delapidated. The drum has had some wear.'

Bullets and Bandsmen

When it was was done the BM was so pleased with the result that he treated Erskine to the Australian cinema nearby. The band was attached to an Australian division while they were here and sometimes joined forces with their brass band.

A sign writing job at Bapaume

'Seemed an incon-gruity to see up-to-date films on what was a little while ago a terrible battle field. It was certainly a 'Casey's Court' picture show. We sat on ammunition boxes for seats.'

One day Erskine and two of the bandsmen, Brewer (who played the cornet) and Powers (the French horn), took a walk over the battlefield,

'....saw the awful havoc of war. Devastation, shell holes, wire, rifles, equipment, rusty, all over the place. Saddest of all the poor remains of men laying about. My first sight of such a thing. Somehow I was more composed than I expected I should be. Mostly Fritzes and Australians here. Been laying there a long time. Quite unrecognisable. The souvenir hunters had already been round.'

The sad remains of war

Crown Copyright, Imperial War Museum

One of Erskine's duties when they were staying near Bapaume was collecting the rubbish. Armed with a sack he would go along the row of tents picking up empty tins and cigarette packets then, carrying his load, trudge along the duck boards to the incinerator where a man stoked the smoking bonfire.

The' Happy Dustman!

On 12 May all thirty members of the band climbed into three GS wagons, each one drawn by half a dozen mules. There were three drivers to each wagon with a corporal on horseback riding alongside. Their destination was Ervillers, a village up near the Line, where they gave a concert for the Artillery. In the audience was a general and his staff, and appropriately in such company the big guns were firing whilst they played. It was a 'swell affair' and they all had a good tea.

The happy dustman

Two days later they were off on their travels again because the 48th Division, and its band, was taking over the camp. They marched back to Ovillers, near Albert, where they had stayed one night

Burning the rubbish

a few weeks earlier; they remained this time for around four days, staying in wooden huts on the chalky field where the bloody advance had taken place in 1916.

Erskine drew a sketch of the temporary billet and sent it home to his father with a letter (post home to Blighty did not require a stamp). He wrote,

16-5-17.

ALBERT. Somme

'...it was a rather uncomfortable place. You could sleep on any old thing you could find - old stretchers, corrugated iron sheets, on the bare ground, as you can observe. Bike belongs to Cyclists' Corps.'

Writing home

Band practice carried on as usual and so did the sign writing jobs, including writing a cross for an officer's grave. One day Erskine walked into the ruined town of Albert where he saw the world - famous Vierge Penchée (or leaning Virgin Mary). On 15 January 1915, a bomb had exploded at the foot of the dome of the Basilique Notre Dame de Brebieres. There had been a statue of the Virgin and Child on top of the tower until the bomb fell when it came off its base and hung perilously to one side. It stayed that way until April 1918.

On 18 May they started a much longer journey, heading north for the Belgian border, to another sector of the Western Front. They marched in the sun with their packs upon their backs as far as the outskirts of Albert, to the railway sidings at Aveluy (the village of that name had been raised to the ground a year earlier). There they boarded the Nord Railway train which would slowly take them the 100 or so kilometres to the frontier with much stopping and starting on the way. Erskine noted,

> 'Passed decent night on the floor of the truck....arrived Bailleul station around
> 9 a.m. in the morning.'

Their belongings on their backs once again, the men marched in the sun a short distance to St Jans Cappel, where the DHQ was putting down its roots for a while. Ahead of them was a full round of playing out engagements.

The billet this time, a loft above some cottages, was more congenial. He wrote,

> 'Poor people's home and they are still living here. Pleasant surroundings'.

As usual they festooned the wall space with their equipment and ranged their instruments round the floor. In the daytime the sunshine poured through a window in the roof.

While they were at St Jans Cappel the band entertained a number of the Division's battalions; men from the South Staffs, the Foresters, the Lincolns, the Dorsets and the Yorks & Lancs. They provided the music for church parades, gave concerts in canteens, and played at the Regimental sports days. They played, too, for the Divisional Train - not the sort that runs on tracks but a group of wagons with officers and men who were responsible for drawing the rations.

— An Idyl.
Flute Versus Clarinet.
W. Jagger. Yorks   L.Cpl. Vickers. Borders

'The country round this locality is magnificent. The trees and fields are lovely including a great number of hopfields which are a feature of the local landscape.'

Less than two weeks later General Haig's new Flanders offensive began; the landscape on the Belgian border would look very different indeed.

Rehearsing when they could

Poperinghe and Talbot House

THE weather was beautiful during the first week in June 1917 and the band piled into the GS wagon practically every day to play for one or other groups of infantrymen. On 7 June the Flanders campaign surged into activity once again and a couple of days later the band was off in the wake of the Division, this time to Dranouter a short distance from the Line. It was warm marching,

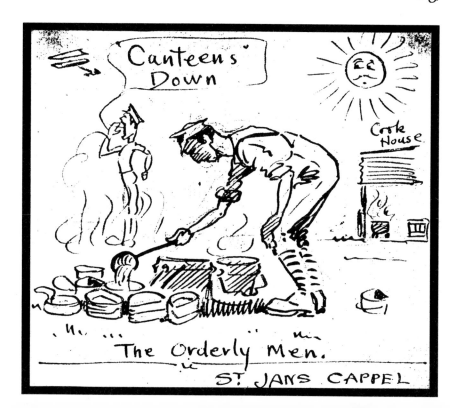

Dishing up the dinner

'Had tunics off being hot...had to fall out...Corporal Stone accompanied me slowly and we fell behind.'

They were some time finding a billet but eventually the band split into groups and moved into several small houses, using a makeshift cookhouse close by. They were now in 'plucky little Belgium', as it had been called at the start of the war. Erskine described Dranouter as 'rather an interesting place.....a few shell holes where Fritz has plonked some souvenirs over recently.'

Suddenly their run of playing out jobs was interrupted by the order to stand by for grave digging fatigue; The Divisional War Diary for 9 June records, '100 casualties sustained by the Division at Wytschaete at the Battle of Messines Ridge.' Erskine had known all along he would be expected to turn his hand to other jobs beside playing the oboe, and short of actually being in the trenches this was the worst he could expect. 10 June was the first day of the burying stint but to his immense relief Erskine was put on duty as standing orderly man, along with Ginger Wood the cornet player; a move which caused 'a bit of bad feeling with a few of the band'. For the time being, at any rate, he had escaped the gruesome task.

Playing selections and songs from the shows continued to be their main occupation - The Bing Boys was showing in the West End of London and its top hit, 'If You Were The Only Girl In The World,' always went down well, a reminder of sweethearts left at home. Their concerts were greatly appreciated by the men they entertained, brightening their lives for a couple of hours. Most had been in the trenches, some were wounded, so badly they would never go back, while others would be returning to the Front.

Keeping clean was almost impossible, even for the men behind the Lines, because baths or showers were few and far between. Uniforms were worn till they were practically falling to bits; on 19 June Erskine observed in his diary,

'Got a new tunic from Quartermaster Schooles - it was time too.'

Practising outdoors - 'Blank hot'

That night, looking smarter than he had been for some time, he played with the band at the Headquarter's Officers' Mess.

The next day everybody packed their things and set off back across the border, making for a French village called Merris, a little to the south west of Bailleul. The band marched but Erskine helped to load the kit and the instruments and travelled all the way by lorry. They set up camp in a convenient field where they stayed for a couple of nights and while they were there they played

En route to a job

outdoors in the village where there were 'plenty of troops about'.

Towards the end of the month the Division moved west for intensive training, to Renescure, 20 kilometres away. This time, instead of travelling by lorry, the band went in a London bus, one of around six hundred that had gone to France to serve as transport for the duration. The glass had been blown out of the windows, which had then been boarded up, so apart from the passengers sitting on top only the driver could see where they were going.

They stayed overnight in Renescure, dossing down in a barn and sleeping on about six feet of straw - 'comfortable - but danger from fire'. The next morning they boarded the bus again ('just room for one on top') and, still travelling west, passed through St Omer en route for the small village of Eperlecques. By now they were less than 30 kilometres from Calais. After much delay the bandsmen were diverted into a field where they put up tents and proceeded to make themselves comfortable. That night they entertained the local residents. Erskine waxed lyrical about this new location.

'Here we have had the best time so far...in a lovely field with a nice clear brook of running water just by our tents to fill the dixies for the cooking.'

While they were at Eperlecques everyone had an inspection for scabies, the cause of intense irritation and scratching. He noted that 'they just look at your chest and between fingers.'

Washing in the field

By now the bandsmen were thoroughly used to playing together and for the next few weeks were out and about practically every day. Sometimes they stood in a market place, sometimes they sat in a hall; the venues varied and on occasions were positively grand, such as the time they played for the officers of the 33rd Brigade in their splendid château HQ at nearby Ganspette.

The 'Wunny Wuns' in action, Eperlecques

Throughout the first three weeks of July there was a flurry of regimental sports in their area and their services were much in demand. These sports days were a wonderful way of forgetting the war and most of the outfits held them. On one occasion, in the same field where their tents were pitched, they played for the Brigade horse show - 'see some good jumping'.

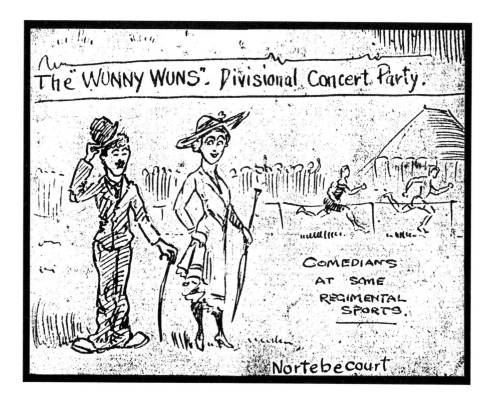

The "WUNNY WUNS". Divisional. Concert. Party.

COMEDIANS AT SOME REGIMENTAL SPORTS.

Nortebecourt

Charlie Chaplin raises his hat at the regimental sports

On 11 July, the day of the 33rd Brigade sports Erskine sent a letter to his father, adding a sketch of a race about to begin. A few days later it was the turn of the Manchesters to hold their sports at Nortbécourt, a village near the Forest of Tournehem. In 1917 Charlie Chaplin was very popular; his films were often shown at the camp cinemas. So one of the Manchesters dressed up as the famous 'tramp', accompanied by an elegantly-clad 'lady'.

On the day of the Manchesters' sports Erskine took a ride on a tank.

'Exciting....was on the top....went down a sharp dip in it.'

In an earlier battle at Pozières in September 1916, when tanks were used for the first time in action, the relentless mud proved too much for them. They were to be used again in the battle of Ypres, which was soon to begin, but it would be at Cambrai on 20 November that they would come into their own.

In mid-July they played for the Divisional Train which at that time was based at Watten, conveniently placed near the main line railway to Calais, where all the supplies from England were landed.

On 22 July the band's last full day at Eperlecques, there were two notable events. At the morning church parade, where they played for the hymns, the sermon was preached by a special visitor, the Bishop of Khartoum. Afterwards at a ceremony on the rifle range the GOC presented Distinguished Conduct Medals and Military Medals to men of the 34th Brigade. The next day they would be heading east, towards the Line, their destination Poperinghe.

The bandsmens' tents were dismantled and their luggage all packed up early on the morning of 23 July. The Divisional Headquarters was moving, too, but instead of going straight to Poperinghe, like the band, it stopped off for a couple of days at Wormhoudt.

The trip went smoothly, the lorry passed through the hilltop town of St Omer, then Cassel and Steenvoorde and over the border to 'Pop'. Nine kilometres further east was Ypres - the soldiers called it Wipers - where there had been two major battles earlier in the war.

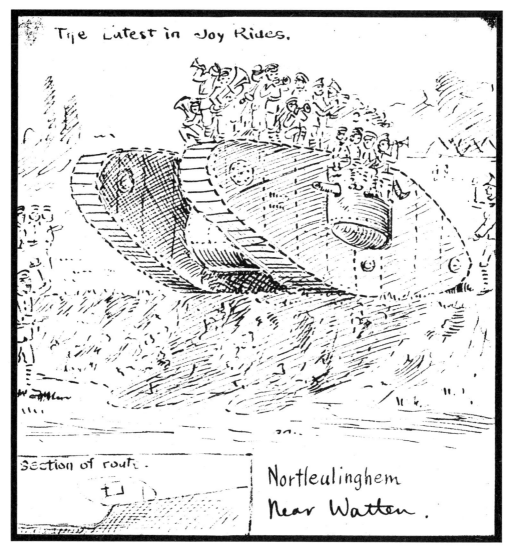

A fanciful sketch of the band

British West Indian Regt.

Seen at 'Pop'

The First Battle of Ypres was in 1914 (19 October - 22 November); for a short time the town was occupied by the Germans. The casualties were horrendous: the British lost 58,000, the French 50,000 and the enemy 130,000. The Second Battle of Ypres was the following year (22 April - 25 May); this time the Germans used poison gas. Their aim was to capture Pilkem Ridge, which they succeeded in doing, but Ypres itself was safe. Again there were huge losses: British 60,000, French 10,000 and Germans 35,000.

As he often commented in his diary, Erskine found the trip from Eperlecques to 'Pop' an 'interesting journey' but he was glad when they arrived in the town and found their billet. This was on the top floor of what had recently been a warehouse, possibly for storing grain, and to reach it they had to climb up a steep ladder.

They slept well that night, thanks to the absence of shelling in spite of the fact that they were now quite close to the Line which was just the other side of Ypres (in turn, 9 kilometres east of 'Pop'). In the morning everybody moved down a floor which was 'somewhat better' and took the opportunity to look around the town which was crawling with soldiers.

Troops came from all over the world

Casualties at a dressing station, Battle of Pilckem Ridge, 31 July 1917

Almost from the very start of the war Poperinghe had been a vital forward base for the Ypres Salient. It was only occupied once and that for a day, in October 1914. It was always a hive of activity, now more so than ever with the battle about to begin. Around the outskirts of the town, in the hopfields, there were depots, training camps and hospitals to receive the wounded; the railway station was a focal point with troops arriving to go to the Front and others going home on leave.

'Pop' was important for another good reason and that was Talbot House, or in signaller's parlance, Toc H. This was a handsome white building with iron doors in Gasthuisstraat which had a sign hanging outside that read 'Talbot House 1915. Every Man's Club'. And that was exactly what it was because officers and men alike could enjoy its hospitality.

It had been decided by the British Army that one of its chaplains should open a club for the troops that would be a haven of retreat from the horrors of war; the man chosen to run it was the Rev. Philip Clayton, known to everybody as 'Tubby'.

Talbot House today

The club, which proved to be an immense success, took its name from a young soldier of 29 who had been killed in July 1915. Gilbert Talbot was the younger brother of Neville Talbot, a senior Army chaplain, and he symbolised the 'golden generation' who were dying on the battlefields.

Erskine and his friends had already heard about Talbot House long before they arrived; he called it 'a sort of church, reading room and canteen'. So that very day, as soon as they had the chance, they went to find it. When they arrived another Divisional band, the 55th, was playing in the garden at the rear and one of the bandsmen was an old chum of Erskine's from England called Wimpenny. He noted,

> 'A good band and quite a treat to hear another.'

They themselves soon got down to practising in a lecture hall attached to Talbot House and the following evening, as he had some time to spare, Erskine accompanied Wimpenny to the 55th Divisional concert party which was called the 'Roses in Melodyland' - 'a capital show with a string band.'

The following day there was yet another change of billet, this time to 'a sort of convent school' with 'good buildings.....plenty of room...tiled floor and a sound roof'. They proceeded to make themelves comfortable, knowing full well that it would only be a matter of time before they received orders to pack up for the next destination. But they were used to that by now.

The courtyard playground of the school was an ideal place for rehearsals. The shells whistled overhead now and then and on one occasion burst in the railway station close by.

> 'It seemed as if it was in the next street...my first experience of shells close to.
> Not nice!'

Erskine's baptism of fire was the first of many times that shells would go whizzing overhead, landing uncomfortably close by.

The garden at Talbot House where the band entertained the troops

On the last day of July the band played in the garden at Talbot House. They had played in some splendid settings in the last few months but this was by far the best. He wrote how it was carefully tended and in many ways a reminder of home; there were tall trees with flowers growing at the base and seats on the lawn where battle-weary soldiers could rest before returning to the Front. On 31 July the 'Northern Operation' (the Third Battle of Ypres) began. The Division belonged to the Fifth Army which was responsible for the plan. The battle ended three and a half months later on   10 November.

Erskine's score card

Essex Farm and the Belgian Frontier

*T*HE Divisional War Diary notes for 1 August 1917, 'A very wet day, making further operations on the front of the Fifth Army almost impossible.' The band's only engagement was entertaining the Lancashire Fusiliers and in the evening Erskine went to a picture show at the camp cinema. The next day could not have been more different.

'The band was employed on a gruesome job today, burying about twenty fellows in the cemetery at Essex Farm. I did my best at digging the one long grave but it gave me my usual headache.

After we had dug the grave at noon we fetched the bodies from the hospital, wrapped in blankets and carried on stretchers. Some were fetched from a makeshift mortuary. There was a whacking great shell hole in the graveyard. Some of the bodies were just as they had been knocked out ...... sights, but the band worked well on the job filling the grave in with earth after a brief service to the accompaniment of screaming shells, some of which were most uncomfortably near...which I'm sure helped to get the hole filled in a lot quicker.

The poor faces at last covered with the earth - what a sad sight. I was moved more by the pitiable appearance of the victims than by the horror of their look. I was surprised to find I could carry one end of a stretcher with its awful load from the hospital to the cemetery; it was a duty which seemed to give me strength....all in drizzling rain.

I had some good pals in the band who did their share of digging and most of mine as well. Let their names be recorded: Ginger Wood, a collier by trade and Haworth, a boiler fireman.'

Erskine and his fellow bandsmen had been dealing with only a tiny fraction of the casualties; the War Diary for 2 August gives a figure of 122 dead (for the Division) and the overall casualties for the '1st Objective' to regain the Ypres Salient   (31 July - 2/3 August) were 31,850. When they had finished burying the dead the bandsmen took their bus back to Poperinghe. The journey was in silence. A few men were let off the burying stint each time it happened and the following day Erskine was among those given a rest.

For two or three days the band returned to giving concerts to the Dorsets, the West Yorks and the Yorkshires. Then came the order for burying of a different kind - not men who had fallen in battle but horses. Some four dozen beasts had been killed by one of 'Fritz's' bombs during an air raid on the Artillery Camp; the gunners had buried many already but it was up to the band to bury the rest.

Ginger Wood. A good pal on grave digging jobs.

'Fortunately the ground is all yellow sand and digs fairly easy. This is heavy work; all the men heave on a rope attached to the animals' fetlocks and drag them into the grave. Great art in getting them in to the best advantage. The legs are broken with blows from an axe so as to take up less room. This job is less gruesome and sad than burying men but the smell of the horses is terrible.

Seemed an incongruity to me to see some of our brilliant musicians bashing away with an axe at the animals' legs, blood all over the place. Our solo cornet seemed to delight in driving a pick into the horses' tummies, much inflated, to puncture them. The job was done to the chief's great satisfaction. We were given a day off owing to having worked so hard.'

Saturday, 11 August was an even more eventful day. That night Erskine wrote in his diary,

'The two burial sergeants came for the band and we went out for the burying, taking the motor bus to within a certain distance of the Line. We walked past Essex Farm (a sinister place) and a long way right into the thick of it, right amongst our field guns.

We divided up into parties but the party I was in got split up and I nearly got lost in the maze of shell holes and broken objects of all descriptions.

Aeroplanes - ours - were overhead and there was a terrible lot of noise from guns all over the shop. I got near to Kitchener Wood, our reserve trenches I believe, and was wandering about when some chaps in a trench told me I was in a dangerous spot and visible from the enemy. The bullets were flying around. So I shifted, met a few of the band and waited behind a concrete emplacement.

Our guns got busy and fired at a rare rate; I could see the countless flashes a long way behind. Some of Fritz's burst round about. We walked back to the spot where we set off (near a pillbox by some artillery), having seen no bodies.

Shells arrived and burst - seemed too close for me - not very nice being under shell fire. We were glad to get back to where we picked up a lorry to get back on. Some of our party had lots to bury but the other lot did nothing.'

X Camp, Peselhoek, near Poperinghe

Conditions at the Front were atrocious - Zillebeke, 9 August 1917

Some of the band went off on another burying stint on the following day and 'got it rather warm' from the shells but Erskine was sent for by the joiners to do a sign writing job. This was at X Camp, near Peselhoek, where the DHQ had moved a week earlier, the band remained in Poperinghe. Erskine moved there with his kit - it was 'much more in my line' than burying.

On Monday 13 August, the band returned to its playing out jobs - just as if nothing had happened and Erskine joined them. One day they were outside playing some cheery tunes for the Northumberland Fusiliers at Siege Camp - 'pretty near the Line' - when an observation balloon was hit by German fire. Fortunately, the observers, who were in the basket hanging beneath, managed to descend safely by parachute. However this little scene took place while the band was in the middle of a piece and they were so amazed by what was happening that the music gradually dried up as they watched!

Erskine found himself doing more and more signwriting work; word had got around that there was a sign writer in camp. Somebody always needed something doing in that line, whether it was a direction board, a sign for a ration dump or a cross with the name, number and regiment of a fallen soldier. He was working with the joiners and wrote,

Officers 1 franc, NCO's 5 centimes, men 3 centimes

'Am in the land of sawdust and shavings now in a funny little stick and mud hut with a corrugated iron roof.'

Though temporarily working as a signwriter, every now and then he was called back to play with the band, which continued to play even though so near to the Line. Variety was the spice of life, in spite of a backdrop of shrapnel and shells.

'Nearly every night see enemy aircraft travelling over us to strafe Poperinghe. Many searchlights and much machine guns and anti-aircraft on the job. Quite exciting... didn't anticipate any bombs being dropped here as it's right in the country and covered in trees. Many shells pass overhead in the night...get quite used to them...some have burst uncomfortably close. Before I came here one went off very near indeed.'

On 24 August he helped load the quartermaster's stores on the lorry and rode with the rest of the tradesmen, as the joiners were called, this time to Border Camp which was situated in a wood of oak trees. There was some problem about finding a hut for them to sleep in; he wrote,

'We were put in and out of a ramshackle hut about four times but eventually were put in a tent.'

Border Camp had a reputation for being 'rather a lively quarter' but nothing much happened while they were there except for the sound of artillery in the distance. A few days later they were moved back again to X Camp - 'Got the old shanty again for our billet'.

During August the DHQ, like Erskine, had moved from one base to another some four or five times: to X Camp, to Border Camp, to Canal Bank (and back to X Camp). During that time the Line was gradually being pushed back, in the direction of Poelcappelle and Paesschendaele. The Division's casualties at the end of the month, recorded in the War Diary, were heavy: Dead: 20 officers, 484 men; Wounded: 74 officers, 1,972 men; Missing: 3 officers, 169 men. It added: Many horses lost.

The billet at X camp, Peselhoek

One day, early in September, Sergeant Taylor, the Bandmaster, called at X Camp to see about Erskine returning to the band full-time. They were actually performing that day at the camp for an officers' football match so he played with them. (It was recorded in the War Diary as a 'quiet day' so they were probably taking advantage of the fact.)

The view from the billet, a result of one of Fritz's shells

The day after he piled his kit into a GS Wagon and got a lift to 'Pop' where the band had been staying all along. He found himself a billet in an empty house, near a church with a very high spire, and that night played for the Duke of Wellington's Regiment. The next day they entertained the Borders, this time at Dirty Bucket Camp where they could hear the shells passing overhead 'to biff the railway station at Pop'.

During their stay in the town there was plenty of attention from Fritz,

> 'Played for the Yorks Regiment here though not a vast audience of troops. Had
> air raid at night, one bomb very near us...shook the building...huge crash.
> Much wind up.'

Most days there was a playing job,

> 'We often get lost trying to find these places, quite a joke amongst the men.
> Played East Yorks today, somewhere in the direction of the Line. They gave
> us a decent tea. We had the old motor bus today - have an exciting passage as
> a rule as the bad roads make it roll excessively.'

Another day they played at the Lincoln's camp at Watou, close to the Belgian Frontier, away from the Line altogether. By contrast to the shells and explosions in the night at least some of the countryside looked charming. They rehearsed every morning and when the weather was fine they played outdoors. On 10 September he recorded,

> 'I struggled through my long passage with the flute accompaniment in William
> Tell.'

Bullets and Bandsmen

One day when they were playing for the West Yorks in the Square at 'Pop' some soldiers firing at a small rifle range provided an extra accompaniment - 'which didn't improve the music'.

September 12 was an important day for Erskine firstly because he had a bath, a luxury that was certainly worth a mention in his diary, and secondly he received some new reeds for his oboe from the bandmaster. That night they played again at Talbot House, which was packed with soldiers enjoying a break from the trenches; the new reeds had come at just the right time because he had a solo to play.

A long way from home - the men of the Chinese labour corps at Poperinghe September 1917

There was another change of billet the following day; back to the old convent where they stayed when they first arrived. The only trouble was that it was next to the Gas School and from time to time they received some 'beautiful whiffs'.

Scenery for the Pierrots - 'a sort of Old Bill gag'

Bullets and Bandsmen

While they were at 'Pop' Erskine was recruited as the 'Wunny Wuns' scene painter. They asked him to paint a battlefield scene for the concert party showing a trench and No Man's Land. Using service green paint on rough canvas he completed it in a couple of days and the end product was 'admired by all.'

Playing out jobs usually ended with a decent meal, whether it was tea in the afternoon or supper in the evening.

> 'We played at the XVIIIth Corps rest camp today near Herzeele, sort of hospital under canvas with convalescent patients. Big audience with a capital tea afterwards. Très bon!'

Later that week because it was too wet to play in the main square in 'Pop' Erskine and a few of his pals went to see another concert party. This was attached to the 55th Division and was called 'The Roses in Melodyland' (their name came from the Divisional badge).

> 'Capital show this...the young 'lady' of the party was indisposed so he didn't appear!'

Around the middle of the month the DHQ moved to Wormhout to the west of Poperinghe and on this occasion the band went there too. After the usual early start they caught the narrow gauge railway there which Erskine described it as a 'sporty ride'. The train ran all the way on the roadside and the soldiers sat in open trucks. As so often happened he felt rather unwell but the billet when they got there was 'fairly comfy, a sort of empty loft or storehouse.' At least it was 'well away from Fritz's attentions'.

Light Rly. Poperinghe to Wormhoudt.

From 'Pop' to Wormhout on the light railway

Sports days were good for the morale for as well as taking the soldiers' minds off things, if only for a while, it also provided excellent exercise. Fitness was important and there were few enough opportunities for the men to keep fit. Sometimes the weather was rotten for the sports, like the drizzly day when the band played for the 34th Brigade events. The next day it was as different again when the band travelled by motor bus to where the Royal Engineers were holding their sports at Dirty Bucket Camp, (called after a nearby farm and almost certainly a corruption of a foreign name). On this occasion the sports were enlivened by the arrival of a 'nice big shell that landed and burst in the next field' but undaunted they carried on with the races as if nothing had happened.

On Saturday, 22 September, another fine day, the Auxiliary Artillery's sports took place at Houtkerque, a Flemish village. Quite often bandsmen Erskine had got to know in Blighty turned up on the Western Front. They were a bit short in the band that day and he wrote,

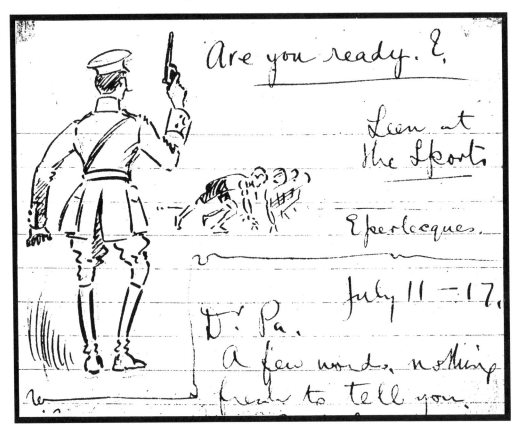

'Gould, an old band chum from the Foresters' band in England, dug me out. Played cornet with us today just for the blow.'

'Are you ready?'

The Division was on the move on 25 September, back to Border Camp, but the band went to Herzeele instead, on the commandeered London bus. 'When you sat upstairs on a rainy day you had to dress accordingly. 'The billet at Herzeele, the next village to Wormhout, was yet another barn.

The London bus used for their engagements

'Our room is in a large loft with a thatched roof and a rare depth of straw on the floor. Frightful risk from fire...chaps lighting fags at intervals all night. A few puffs then pinch them out.'

The day after their arrival they rehearsed al fresco in a field - 'very pleasant' - and later took the bus to 'Pop' where they played once again in the Talbot House garden. For their concert at the XVIIIth Corps Rest Camp at Herzeele they spent extra time rehearsing; one of the pieces, 'Reminiscences of Verdi', was proving difficult. However, when they took their seats in the marquee and started to play it was 'alright on the night' and they were rewarded with a slap-up tea.

While training continued behind the Line, which was now moving further to the east, the infantry and artillery were fighting at the Battle of Polygon Wood. The War Diary notes, 'Care should be taken that the number of wounded reported should not be exaggerated....very few found dead.' It also stresses the importance of burying all dead bodies found near the Lines 'not only for sanitary reasons but for morale also.'

Towards the end of the month the band changed their musical programme, they had quite a repertoire by now, and Erskine made some sketches. There was one more playing job at the XVIIIth Corps Rest Camp, 'where they do us so well.' Then suddenly, on 2 October, they were on the move again, loading the London bus with their instruments and packs. There was no room for them as well as their gear, so they started off for Border Camp the best way that they could.

After marching part of the way they caught the little roadside train they had travelled in before, then transferred to an open truck, sitting on top of a load of granite stones. There was more marching and three separate lorry rides before they finally arrived at the Camp. No comfortable barn awaited them there, just tents in the middle of a field.

When they arrived Erskine felt dreadful. His head was throbbing; he was physically sick and couldn't eat a thing. The only thing that cheered him up was that they were able to listen to the 48th Divisional Band ('a treat') who were playing that day.

A fellow bandsman polishes his trombone in the billet at Herzeele

He wrote in his diary,

> 'This spot has an evil reputation...many air raids. This evening a Taube came over and dropped a bomb on the Camp quite close to the bus, which set fire to it and burnt everything inflammable. Burst with huge flare for a long time...great sight. Both the drivers were injured and taken away, with one of the band who was there at the time. Bus driver's dog injured also.'

All that remained when a bomb hit their bus

The band thought they had been moved to Border Camp for more burying duties but to everyone's relief discovered they were probably going to guard the rapidly growing numbers of prisoners of war. 'Much wind up', Erskine added to the diary, 'but we eventually got to sleep.'

The Division was involved in two more important battles that month in the Ypres Salient - Broodseinde on the 4th and Poelcappelle on the 9th. (Then followed the two Battles of Passchendaele which were fought over the most appalling ground conditions on 12 October and then again 26 October - 10 November.) The total British casualties from 31 July - 10 November were 244,897; the German casualties (possibly) 400,000.

On 23 October there was a change of plan and the Division, and the band, some in a lorry and some by train, headed south to another sector; their destination was Bracquemont, near the mining town of Noeux-les-Mines. They would remain there until Christmas and then return the following year for an even longer stay; the band and the 'Wunny Wuns' would get to know the area very well indeed.

Noeux-les-Mines

WITHIN a day or so of arriving at Bracquemont, where the DHQ was established in a château, the band resumed its playing jobs. They played to the Divisional Train, the 33rd and 34th Ambulance, the Yorks, the Borders, the Canadian Artillery and many other units, rehearsing as often as they could so that they could vary their programme.

'Samson and Delilah' was one of their latest pieces and, in complete contrast, a medley of Irish folk songs which had a solo passage for Erskine's oboe. Occasionally one of Fritz's shells landed whilst they were playing, but they were quite used to that by now. They performed in all sorts of venues in and around Béthune; hospital wards, YMCA canteens, bandstands in parks and village squares. Mostly the audience was appreciative and of good size but they had their share of playing to a lone villager, a few children and a dog.

Going to the pictures was one of Erskine's favourite pastimes; photography was another, but cameras weren't allowed on the Western Front. While he was in Noeux-les-Mines, which was just up the road from the château, he and his pals often visited the little town's cinema, the Noeuxois. The Divisional cinema, even when full of soldiers expressing themselves freely, was positively tranquil compared with the Noeuxois. He wrote,

'The kids behave like hooligans, perfect pandemonium between the films.'

In 1917 the cinema was still in its infancy and the Talkies had not yet arrived; there were few language problems for the soldiers to overcome. The actors and actresses relied on their performances to put the story across and the captions were fairly easy to follow for a soldier with a smattering of French. However in spite of the din they still went to the Noeuxois to see some different films.

About this time Erskine received a letter from Tommy (Ginger) Wood, who had been such a tower of strength on the burying jobs. Ginger was now in a convalescent camp and 'badly in need of fags', an essential aid to recovery.

Deflandre, édit., Hautmont

Rue Nationale, Noeux-les-Mines

For 18 November the War Diary notes, 'Enemy shelled our Reserve Line fairly heavily during morning' and three days later '2nd Coy 7/South Staffs got lost - 1 officer and 40 other ranks killed, 6 missing and 28 wounded.'

This was also the time of the Battle of Cambrai, 45 kilometres to the south-east, where after two abortive attempts in earlier battles the new-fangled tank finally came into its own. At Cambrai there was an attempt to breach the barbed wire and trenches of the famous Hindenburg Line. It produced enormous casualties, about 44,000 British and 53,000 German. Though the tanks did succeed in bursting through there was no outright winner because within a fortnight the British were almost back to square one. However this did not stop the initial impact of the tanks from being hailed as a victory and the bells were rung in London the following day. From then on 20 November has been the Royal Tank Regiment's regimental day.

Ginger Wood plays his cornet

With Christmas so near some of the men were anxious to learn if they were going to have any leave. Some were lucky; one of the Lance Corporals went on a pass and so did Sergeant Taylor, the Band Master. Erskine wrote, 'I'm expecting mine very soon.'

Sergeant Taylor conducts the Divisional band

A Padre enjoys the Show.

Comic Pierrot

Major King and a Pierrot from the 'Wunny Wuns'

One day a cement floor was being put in their rehearsal hut so Erskine used the time to pay a much-needed visit to the barber in the town; a short back and sides was essential in the interests of cleanliness. Later that day he was fetched from his billet and told to report to the Pierrots, where he was interviewed by a lieutenant and the chaplain, Major King, who was the leading light in the concert party.

They told him they needed his help on an urgent job, painting four, or possibly five, sets of scenery for their forthcoming pantomime. He wrote,

'Am off band jobs till this is done. It is a very tall order.'

As soon as he could he walked into town, found a shop selling artists' materials and bought some brushes and paint. This job was going to take up most of his time for the next few weeks and he wondered if he would get his long awaited spell of leave.

It was important to find a suitable place where he could work, somewhere he could leave the scenery each night and be sure to find it safe and sound the following morning. Eventually he found the ideal spot, a partitioned off section in the 7th Casualty Clearing Station (which doubled as cinema and theatre) where he could work uninterrupted. He found some canvas about four feet wide and joined the sections together (the total width of the back drop was eighteen feet across). A young lance-corporal called Jock, from the Labour Company, was seconded to him as handy-man assistant. Between them they mixed the distemper for priming the canvas before applying the paint for the background.

When Erskine heard about the job he made some rough designs for the scenery and showed them to the Lieutenant for his approval. He returned to the shop in the town and, after a struggle to make himself understood, came away with more colours and a few extra brushes. He spent the first day, a Monday, working on Cinderella's Kitchen and in the evening pinned up the canvas for the Forest Scene.

While he was working on the scenery he moved from the band billet and lived for the duration with the concert party, sleeping in the part of the theatre which had been partitioned off. Here at least it was warm and he was comparatively comfortable. What's more they messed at a private house where Madame cooked the food, which according to Erskine was 'très bon'.

On Wednesday, December 12, Erskine was summoned and told he could go on leave that very morning, which in the ordinary way would have been good news indeed. He explained to the officer that he was committed to finishing the scenery and arranged instead to go when the job was done. He was in a dilemma, naturally he wanted to go home and visit his father but he had a job to finish ready for the pantomime's opening night. When he returned to his 'studio' he made a start on the Corridor Scene; that evening there was a particularly heavy air raid. He wrote,

'Some came very close...much wind up.'

The Divisional War Diary notes, that 'enemy airplanes flew low over our Lines and dropped bombs in the evening.'

Erskine reckoned that if all went well it would take him about a week to finish the scenery, using all kinds of makeshift materials. From time to time his pals from the band and the officer-in-charge, would pop in and watch him at work and pass the time of day. The Corridor Scene, which was used while the sets were changing, involved painting three 'ancestral' portraits. There were eight side wings to do, as well as the back drop for the Palace scene, so he still had a heavy workload.

One evening he took a break from his painting and went to watch the concert party, the men wearing their traditional Pierrot suits with pom-poms and ruffles round their necks. There was a good house for the two-hour show and Erskine, like the rest of the audience, thoroughly enjoyed it.

By 15 December he had completed the Corridor and though, personally, he thought the portraits were 'jolly rough' it was 'widely acclaimed'. By now he had run out of canvas and could not move on to the Palace scene so he spent another night at the Pierrots, who were playing this time to the background music of Fritz, who was operating from the air somewhere in the vicinity. There was still no canvas the following day, which meant further delays, however his pal Simpson, back from leave in Blighty, brought Erskine a letter from home which cheered him up somewhat. He wrote in his diary, 'Pa, delighted at the prospects of a leave.'

This building served as a church, cinema and theatre

Dispatch Rider.

Nov. 1917

An army dispatch rider seen near Noeux-les-Mines

Snow began to fall just a week before Christmas - it looked just like a greetings card - and morning ablutions were 'a time of great fortitude'. There was still no canvas for the scenery and Erskine's chances of getting home for the holiday were slowly fading. He wrote,

'It seems as if something is purposely delaying the canvas.'

But in his heart he knew there must be a perfectly good explanation - after all, there was a war on. To fill in time he made some sketches of the concert party to send home to his father, watched another boxing match and, with Simpson, visited the tiny 'dust hole' cinema.

At last, on 19 December, a freezing cold day, the canvas arrived, from a theatre at nearby Mazingarbe. This meant he could start the Palace scene, drawing the outlines of the larger sections leaving Jock, his assistant, to fill them in with paint. That night he went to see another concert party; this was the 'Whizz Bangs' of the 46th Division who had a string band providing the music and 'gave a decent show'.

Outside 'every twig was outlined with hoar frost' but in the warmth of the theatre work continued apace on the Palace scene. When that was finished he still had to paint the Library Scene, plus four sets of wings. His pass home for Christmas now seemed most unlikely and, not unnaturally, he was very disappointed.

Erskine fetches the water at Noeux

Two of the Pierrots, who belonged to the Royal Army Medical Corps, gave Erskine and Jock a hand with the Library scene to help them get it finished and two days before Christmas it was finally done. Then word came that they were about to make a move, 'sometime tomorrow', as the hall was to be taken over by men of Princess Patricia's Canadian Light Infantry.

Erskine was now resigned to the fact that he would be spending Christmas in France but with any luck he would be going on leave early in the New Year. He had already had a card from his brother Frank and no doubt a parcel from home was on its way.

All packed up and ready to go, the Pierrots waited all day for the lorries to take them to their next destination, but to nobody's great surprise the transport never arrived. This was always happening so they resigned themselves to another night in their billet; but come what may, they had to be out by tomorrow ready for the next arrivals to move in.

> 'We had final meal at Madame's where we get our food....quite upset at our farewell...much embracing. These people think a lot of the concert party. Tomorrow is Christmas Day. The second that I've had out here.'

25 December was hectic. The Canadian Division were taking over, so in the morning they cleared out all their stuff from the hall and packed it up in a nearby hut. Then 'most carefully' swept up the main hall and delivered it over to the incoming concert party. Now of 'no fixed abode' they moved, temporarily, into the attic of 7th Casualty Clearing Station where the men of the RAMC had their quarters.

> 'We were all invited to the Christmas Dinner given for the officers and staff of the hospital. It was a grand affair, very swell, with turkey, plum pudding etc, and we all enjoyed it immensely. The tables and the rooms were beautifully decorated.'

Spreading the word

SPEED
NOT TO
EXCEED
12 M.P.H.

OUR
MOTOR BUS
DRIVER

A.S.C

Pop.

After the meal the 'Wunny Wuns' gave a concert and later in the afternoon put on an impromptu show for the wounded soldiers in the wards. Everybody's thoughts were with their relatives and friends at home but the entertainment helped to keep their spirits up. That night Erskine and the Pierrots slept in the spacious attic; tomorrow they would be on the move.

On Boxing Day the snow lay thick on the ground and after breakfast in the Mess with the men from the Medical Corps, the Pierrots packed up their stage fittings ready to leave. Before they left they gave one more concert for the wounded. Erskine wrote,

'The poor chaps in the ward are in a bad way.'

Finally the long-awaited transport arrived and after tea, provided by the hospital sisters, they loaded up the transport and set out on a cold moonlight drive to Labeuvrière, a few kilometres west of Béthune, where the DHQ had gone on ahead.

The motor bus driver

They encountered the usual delay on arrival but after dumping their luggage at the Divisional Train, they finally found their billet - a dilapidated old barn. Compared to the trenches, though, it was a palace and what's more they were not quite as close to the Line as they had been. The day after they arrived they fixed up a messing arrangement with a woman in a nearby house so they would be able to have regular meals. Erskine knew this area well as he had often played there with the band.

As soon as he could he resumed work on the scenery, setting up a makeshift workshop in the barn. He managed to find a joiner and arranged to have the side wings made, ready for him to paint. The Pierrots got the stage ready for a performance that night but some of the party were unwell; two of them had severe colds and 'Rosie' the female impersonator was unable to go on.

Corporal Philpotts alias Rosie

Dorset Regt

OuR Female "Impostor."

Corpl. Philpotts   from life

Bullets and Bandsmen

That evening the cinema party, and some of the luggage, caught up with the Pierrots. The bandsmen arrived the following day. The bandmaster asked Erskine when he would be joining them again; he said he hoped it would not be long as the scenery was nearly finished. It was certainly coming on: the joiner had fashioned the framework for the side wings so that Erskine could cover them with canvas. Firth, the cinema operator, rigged up an acetylene lamp so that he could work in the evening as well.

On 30 December a thaw set in and there was water dripping everywhere. Erskine noted in his diary that the French ink he was using was very thin. New Year's Eve was as cold as it had been before the thaw and his fingers were numb as he tried to paint. He wrote,

> 'Can't put much interest in the job under these conditions. The colour begins to freeze on the scenery.'

At 3 p.m. he decided to call it a day and went instead in the lorry with the Pierrot boys to assist them at a show. As they approached Béthune they got caught in a raid with bombs bursting near them and shrapnel falling close to the lorry. He wrote,

> 'Awful. Don't like it at all.'

When they arrived at the hall they found the concert had been cancelled, so they turned back for Labeuvrière where bombing continued throughout the night.

Blighty and Back

IN 1914 they had said it would all be over by Christmas but here was January 1918 and neither side had won. Erskine wrote in his new diary,

'The New Year dawns and no sign of peace.'

Visitors called at the house where they messed throughout New Year's Day to wish Madame and Mademoiselle the compliments of the season. There was much kissing on both cheeks by the relations and handing out of centimes to the children.

With the help of his assistant and also some of the Pierrots Erskine started fixing up the scenery in the recreation hall-cum-theatre where they were going to present Cinderella. Meanwhile working by candlelight in the draughty barn he continued to finish the rest of the scenery. At last he noted, 'The good job well done.' Erskine could now look forward to the leave he had to forego in the interests of painting the scenery.

There were dozens of different concert parties like the 'Wunny Wuns', performing all over the Western Front, attached to armies, corps, divisions and brigades, even to field ambulance units. Their names used to reflect their insignia, their work or where they came from. There were the 'Verey Lights' (1st Corps), the 'Black Diamonds' (29th Division), the 'Roses' (55th Division), the 52nd 'Thistle Tops' and the 1st Army's 'Rouge et Noir'. From the other side of the world came the ANZAC 'Coves' and from Canada the 'Maple Leaves' and the 'Dumb Bells'.

Erskine listed nearly 70 different troupes in the back of his diary, including the 'Swifts' and the 'Soarers' (appropriately from the Royal Flying Corps), the 'Whizz Bangs', the 'Shell Shifters' and the 'Snipers'. He noted that the 6th Division's 'Fancies' had been captured. There was a great deal of talent on the Western Front on both sides of No Man's Land; the Germans had their concert parties and military bands as well.

About this time it was decided that the Pierrots should have a small string orchestra of their own with musicians drawn from the Divisional Band. Erskine would be playing the violin. The day this was announced he heard that at long last his leave pass had come through so, after a talk with Major King, it was agreed that while he was in London he would visit a certain music shop and select some extra instruments for the orchestra.

Saturday 5 January, was the great day; for the first time in over a year he was finally going on leave. He started out on foot from Labeuvrière to Chocques where he caught a motor to the railway station at Lillers. Then it was by train all the way, via Béthune and Etaples, finally arriving at Boulogne, which as usual was crowded with servicemen. Erskine made for a billet where, armed with blankets and bed boards, he made himself as comfortable as he could for the night.

Our Pianist

'The Wunny Wuns' pianist

Next morning, after a wash-and-brush-up and a shave, he had a bite to eat. It was the middle of the afternoon before the ferry (the 'London') finally left the quay but to his relief the Channel crossing was pleasantly smooth and when they berthed in Folkestone he caught a quick train up to Victoria. It was then just a matter of catching a tram to Tooting where 'Poor Pa' (as his children often called him) was quite delighted to see him.

It was wonderful to be home again, to catch up on the news and talk ten to the dozen to his family and friends; everybody was pleased to see him and hear what he had to say. On 8 January he went into town to Butterfields, the music shop, to order the instruments for the Pierrots' little orchestra; the only one they could not provide was the cello. Later in the day he visited some of his relatives at the Borough and gave his father a hand with some signwriting, talking all the while about his experiences in France.

His brother Charley came to visit them the following day, with little Jack his son. They paid a flying visit to see yet more relations, this time at Greenwich, and the adults went to see a show at the Alhambra called 'Round the Map' ; Erskine thought it 'rather slow'.

For a short while Erskine was back in the old routine helping his dad in the workshop. One day after writing a couple of coffin plates he set out for Sutton where Jess, his

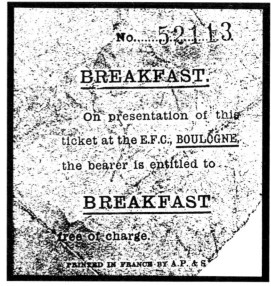

Erskine's breakfast ticket

eldest sister, lived with her husband Jim, who was also on leave from the Army. He took the omnibus to Mitcham and walked the rest of the way in the pouring rain (after trudging along so many muddy roads in France this was no problem at all). They were both delighted to see him and hear all his news.

On his return to Tooting he found a telegram from Major King, who was also in Blighty, asking to meet him the following day at the music shop. There they selected two fiddles and a viola, a double bass, a drum and a glockenspiel on which the Major left a deposit, then Erskine bought himself a cup of coffee in the nearest Lyons tea shop.

Saturday 19 January was his last day on leave so he made the most of the time that was left by visiting some friends, including a Mrs Petrie whose husband had been reported missing in France. Lizzie, his stepmother - the third Mrs Williams - gave him a pocket book to take back with him. Everyone waved him off as he set out for Victoria where he found a bed for the night in the Salvation Army hostel. On Sunday morning he was roused at 5 a.m. and ate a filling breakfast in the Sally Army canteen (price elevenpence). At 6.30 a.m. he caught the train to Folkestone, as usual packed with servicemen weighed down with kit, and on arrival marched about a mile to a large empty house where he stayed until the ferry came in.

It was dusk by the time the 'Invicta' left the quayside and after a windy crossing Erskine embarked at Boulogne. Then he marched up to St Martin's Camp where, after drawing two blankets and drinking a welcome 'cupper', he retired for the night in a crowded hut, ready for an early rise. It was early; reveille was sounded at 1.30 a.m.! Breakfast came soon after and Erskine wrote in his new diary,

'It was a change to get food freely, after the shortage in Blighty'.

He managed to get a 'decent third class carriage' on the train from Boulogne Station and travelled east via St Pol to Chocques, walking the rest of the way to Labeuvrière where he ate a midday meal with the Band, had a shave and a short nap. He was certainly glad to get to bed that night.

The next day it was as if he had never been away. Sergeant Taylor the bandmaster had returned to his regiment and Sergeant Pullinger, no friend of Erskine's, was now in charge of the band. There was no rehearsal that day as they were off on their travels again tomorrow so he had yet more sleep on his 'fairly comfortable' wire bed in the barn. He noted,

> 'We have our food in better style here, proper mess room in an estaminet near the band billet.'

On the morning of 23 January, the DHQ was on the move again, travelling East to Sailly Labourse, a village south-east of Béthune. Reveille was called at 4.30 a.m., another early morning for Erskine. After a hurried breakfast the band left Labeuvrière on foot in the dark and marched to the station at Chocques where they caught the train to Béthune. They were now getting closer to the Line and completed their journey partly by truck and partly on foot. The billet at Sailly was another derelict barn; Erskine was appointed Orderly Man as soon as they arrived, his duty to help draw the rations.

Great preparations were in hand the following day because the band was going to play at the coast. They and their kit needed to be immaculate.

Bandmaster Pullinger

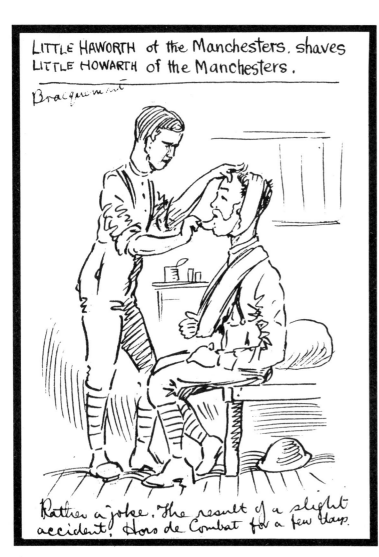

LITTLE HAWORTH of the Manchesters, shaves LITTLE HOWARTH of the Manchesters.

Bracquemont

Rather a joke. The result of a slight accident! Hors de Combat for a few days.

They were up at 6 a.m. on the day of their trip and once again ate breakfast while it was still dark. Two GS wagons turned up to take the band part of the way. They were headed west for Boulogne, where Erskine noted 'Fritz had been up'. They slept that night in the station, in the railway wagon that had completed their journey. The following morning, not without some difficulty, they managed to cook their rations for breakfast.

They waited for the lorry to take them to their destination, the 1st Army Training School at Hardelot, about 10 kilometres to the south, but there was no sign of it for hours. They spent most of the day at the YMCA - and noted the presence of the WAACs, girls of the Women's Auxiliary Army Corps who were a welcome new phenomenon in time of war. Finally a lorry and a bus did turn up - at 6 p.m. - and they all piled in for a bumpy journey to the training school, where they were given a plate of stew and cup of tea before turning in for the night.

A wash and brush up

Their billets for the stay at Hardelot were two bow huts in a clearing among the pine trees. The day after they arrived Erskine and his pal Simpson went for a walk through the wood to the shore; this made a pleasant change from the battle-scarred countryside where they usually stayed. That afternoon the band played for a football match and though it was the end of January the weather was more like spring.

The château where the training school had its HQ was a splendid building, like so many other châteaux that had been commandeered by the BEF for the duration. The week at Hardelot was hectic. Every morning they played on the lake-side parade ground for morning inspection. Then throughout the day, they provided martial music while officers and men marched up and down on the various training grounds. Erskine wrote,

'These parades are wonders of military smartness and precision.'

Walking out in the pinewoods

E. S. 909. ~~Hardelot (P. de C.)~~ — Le Château
Emplacement d'un Château-Fort restauré en 1223 par
Philippe-le-Hurepel, comte de Boulogne; fut habité par
Henri VIII, roi d'Angleterre, et detruit en 1668 par de
Campaigno.

The château at Hardelot, on the back of the postcard it reads 'passed by censor'

One afternoon they went by bus to the hospital on the front to help cheer the wounded with their music; afterwards they were given a delicious tea, a perk they always enjoyed. One evening they played in the Sergeants' Mess and another time gave a concert for the officers, when 'many WAACs were present'.

While he was at Hardelot Erskine sometimes changed his oboe for the cymbals ('getting quite hot at them'). The bandsmen did have some free time to themselves while they were at the coast - and the opportunity to get to know the WAACs.

On their last morning at the Training School the band accompanied some Canadian infantry on a circular route march, playing all the while. Their brief but enjoyable stay at Hardelot ended on 3 February. The weather had turned much colder with ice on the water in the wash house. After breakfast a lorry took them to Boulogne station where they caught the train back to Béthune - and close to the Line.

A lorry waiting at the station took their luggage on to the billet at Sailly Labourse while they marched 'at a terrific rate'. There were mugs of tea on arrival and a clutch of letters from home, the first Erskine had received since he was back in France.

The following day the band rehearsed the music for the Pierrots' pantomime and that evening played for the first performance, watched by the General and a group of officers. The show was voted a great success. Meanwhile the instruments that Erskine and the Major had chosen arrived from England. The next day the string orchestra, which included Erskine, started to practise.

Erskine played the cymbals at Hardelot

The Eb Clarinet.

L.Cp. Bradley.   6th Borders

'Everybody blowing or scraping...
I've been having a go on one of the
fiddles and have a tutor to practise
from. Seems to come back to me,
although not touched a violin for a
long time.'

That evening the panto was cancelled as
there was no electric light. So instead the
Pierrots presented their usual concert party
show. While they were singing a heavy
bombardment began, Erskine noted,

'We were dispersed by an officer
but fortunately there were no
injuries...had a very narrow escape
last night.'

The next night the light was back on again
and so was 'Cinderella'. All ranks enjoyed the
show and so did a critic from a theatrical
journal of the day. This is what he wrote,

The E flat clarinet

DIVISIONAL PANTO IN THE DANGER ZONE

It is scarcely within range of Fritz's guns that one would look for dainty fairies and shimmering grottoes, dazzling ballrooms and elegant footmen, and such like pantomime paraphernalia. But the concert party of the 11th Division have (writes J.W.O., a journalist who is now doing his bit in France) been presenting nightly within the danger zone their Christmas pantomime of 'Cinderella' with an elaborateness nothing short of marvellous. Coloured limelight effects and a change of scenery, beautiful dresses and a large orchestra, all serve to render the production very little behind the average panto in 'Blighty'.

This is largely due to the fact that the 11th Division contains within its ranks not only first-class fighting men, veritable 'storm troops', but first-class entertainers as well, who have had practical experience of catering for music hall devotees all over the British Isles. The stage manager is Lieutenant Cecil Field, late acting manager of the Hammersmith Palace, whose many friends in the vaudeville world will be happy to learn that his talents have found so useful and congenial a channel.

Female characters must needs be impersonated by males but no difficulties have been encountered in this direction. As Cinderella Corporal Philpotts (stage name Percy St Clair) is thoroughly at home, he having toured the music halls of Blighty as 'The Immaculate Lady' and worn petticoats professionally for ten years.'

The review ended,

'Altogether, the 'Wunny Wuns', as the concert party of the 11th Division is called, are as clever as they are versatile.'

Bullets and Bandsmen

Erskine wrote on the last night of the pantomime,

> 'The Pierrots let themselves go with much mirth that wasn't in the book, to the delight of one and all.'

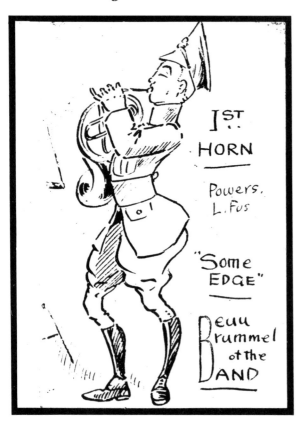

1ST HORN

Powers. L. Fus

"Some EDGE"

Beau Brummel of the Band

Now that their instruments had arrived from England the new string orchestra practised daily and in early February were joined by a violinist from the Border Regiment who had played in the 33rd String Orchestra. Erskine accompanied the new arrival in some violin duets and they in turn were accompanied by the sound of falling shells. The Divisional War Diary notes, 'Our artillery fired on working parties and Howitzers and engaged hostile trench mortars' - clearly Fritz wasn't having it all is own way.

A day or so later the orchestral parts turned up as well so now they could practise the pieces that they were going to play, with Erskine on first fiddle alongside the man from the Borders.

Sunday 10 February, after playing at church parade the band travelled by lorry to Vaudricourt where their audience consisted mainly of men of the Chinese Labour

Beau Brummel of the Band

Company. This time, ever versatile, Erskine played the oboe and found the occasion 'quite a novelty....went well'. Unfortunately he did not record what sort of music they played for these men who were so very far from home!

Throughout 1918, in his Letts's 'Quikref' diary, Erskine kept a careful note of his Army pay, which was usually handed out once a fortnight. This was about 10 francs a week, the exchange rate was then 25 francs to the pound. He also kept a record of when he lent money to his pals which was sometimes as little as one franc or as much as fifteen. As they paid him back he crossed off their names. There was very little to spend his money on apart from smokes and toiletries; unlike most of the other bandsman he rarely went out on the town, so he was always 'good for a touch'.

One afternoon, to the sound of their own artillery, they had their first proper rehearsal playing as an orchestra instead of a military band. 'No fresh Paganini's on the scene as yet' he noted in his diary but Lieut. Field (the officer mentioned in the review) and Major King both thought they were progressing rather well.

In mid-February the enemy gunfire increased, a fact confirmed in the Divisional War Diary, which also notes that numerous enemy balloons, carrying 'propagandist papers', had come down in the front line trenches and rear areas of the Division. Written in English these missives were a fairly common occurrence, showering down and often announcing a gas attack as a 'retaliatory measure'. Erskine observed after one such warning, 'It didn't come off.'

Sunday, 17 February was Erskine's 37th birthday. There was no mention of presents in his diary, only that another new violinist had joined the orchestra, this time from the Yorks Regiment. That evening, because it was a special occasion, he paid a shilling 'in a sort of private house shop' for a celebratory plate of eggs and a cup of coffee.

Mail and bunches of newspapers came fairly regularly from home, keeping them up-to-date with the news in other theatres of war. Things began to hot up towards the end of the month and on 25 February Erskine wrote,

'Fritz been at it again. At 5 o'clock sent a salvo over in region of the cinema. Rare bunch of shells. Killed child just coming out of school and wounded others...our guns very busy.'

Kirkham - a trombone player with little feet

That evening the concert party show was cancelled because the electric wires had been cut in the raid. And anyway nobody had much enthusiasm after the tragedy at the school. The next afternoon, when the bandsmen were returning from their rehearsal to their billet, at around 4 p.m. they were caught in a salvo of shellfire.

'Laid down near the wall....lucky escape.'

After that they quite expected Fritz to send over more the following day, and even left off their practice to avoid it. They were quite prepared for it when some field gun shells came their way.

'Only lasted a few minutes but it was very warm...fortunately no one was hurt.'

By now it was March, and Erskine was still waiting for his own violin to arrive from home. His brother Frank had tried to post it to him but found it was overweight. Then he had a bright idea: he arranged that Kirkham, the trombonist, should collect it from Frank when next he went on leave in the Midlands. Meanwhile he continued to use a borrowed instrument.

Towards the end of the previous month the DHQ had moved on from Sailly to Verquin, but the band was not to follow on until the middle of March. The weather was bitterly cold, it was snowing and there was a biting wind but the band hardly noticed because they were busy rehearsing indoors. They were all looking forward to the first time their small orchestra would play for a church service but when the day came, to their dismay, it was cancelled. (A 'wash-out' in military parlance.)

To make matters worse, at noon, there was 'a severe spasm' of shelling from Fritz when two of the shells fell uncomfortably close to their billet. 'Rather unpleasant', said Erskine, who was given to understatement. That afternoon the full military band piled into the lorry and played at the 33rd Field Ambulance in Fouquières, the other side of Béthune, to lighten the lives of the wounded. In comparison with their plight the bandsmen had very few worries indeed.

Pte. Jackson,

'Cello

from life.

Private Jackson the cello player

Meanwhile they had other duties to carry out, such as erecting a splinter-proof barrier around the camp cinema; it was about a yard high and Erskine helped fill the wheelbarrows with the earth which was packed into sandbags. Hardly a day passed without the sound of 'our' artillery and the sight of flashes in the sky. Erskine wrote,

'Thought of the chaps in the Line.'

Although he was not an infantryman he had heard from the soldiers who had been there what life and death was like in the trenches, and of course he had seen for himself the stricken landscape, the craters and the ever-present mud. He also had great admiration for those villagers who remained in their homes - 'they stick it very well.'

After a morning working on the cinema's protective barrier the orchestra travelled to Verquin to play for the Pierrots' concert party where once again 'they had a warm time' - and he wasn't referring to the weather.

On their return to Sailly they heard that there had also been heavy shelling in their absence.

On Sunday 10 March, the string band finally made its debut, playing for the church service in the Divisional canteen. Then, after they had eaten, they were off again to Fouquières, playing again for the wounded, but this time it was only the weather that was warm and they played outdoors in the sun. After they had eaten the customary 'thank you ' tea they returned back via Béthune, where they saw for themselves the appalling devastation of the air raids. On 13 March he noted,

> 'Two years ago I started soldiering at Brocton. Didn't think it would have
> lasted all this time.'

That night they played 'a good number of songs' for the Pierrots over at Verquin and arrived back at the billet just in time for the shelling to start. There was very little sleep for anyone that night and, to make matters worse, all the power lines were down. Sailly was now almost deserted and even the stoical villagers were leaving.

The next morning Erskine heard that he must attend a Medical Board, along with 'a few lame ducks of the band', and if they did not pass this fitness test they were going to be transferred to the Labour Company. Whatever the outcome of the Board, though, he would continue to play with the band.

The Medical Board was held at La Motte, a small village tucked into the Forêt de Nieppe. Captain Edwardes accompanied Erskine and the other three members of the band on the trip. When they got there all they had to do was answer a few questions put to them by the Doctor. Everybody expected to be passed B1 but as to when they would know for certain, well, it could be at any time.

The formalities out of the way, they all went back to Sailly where the band was due to a start a short tour of the area, playing (and staying) that first night at Verquin, where the DHQ was already established. This village was slightly further from the shelling than Sailly but they still received a visit from the droning Taubes on the night they arrived.

Inside the billet at Verquin

St Patrick's Day, 17 March, began with a church service, in one of the huts. There was a flurry of excitement as Fritz began firing shrapnel at a nearby observation balloon, with some 'very loud reports'. This particular Sunday was also the day they received their pay so the band bought some chips at a nearby house. Erskine wrote,

> 'These people make quite a trade of fried spuds.'

The concert tour continued with a visit to Aire-sur-la-Lys, an attractive old town. Here, for their short stay, the bandsmen were billeted in rooms above an estaminet and their audience that night, in the Hôtel de Ville, was composed almost entirely of officers from the nearby Instruction Camp.

There was much alarm on the day they left Aire because Fritz had called in the night and one of his shells had wrecked three houses, injuring a number of people. Fortunately no one had been killed and as Erskine learned afterwards it was the first time the town had been shelled.

When they got to Verquin, their next destination, they had quite expected to give a show but they found instead that another concert party (from a different

The 11th Divisional Orchestra; Erskine second left with the violin

division) had been booked to appear instead. So, having nothing else to do, they sat down and watched it. He noted, 'Not bad.' That night Béthune, just a little further north was heavily bombed, so nobody had much sleep.

The band was now back with DHQ. The War Diary mentions the heavy bombardment of the previous nights and evidently some slackness had been observed because Thursday 22 March began with an inspection, with rifles, by the Company Commander. That same day the Divisional orchestra had their photograph taken with their instruments, their officer (as always in such formal pictures) sitting in the centre of the front row. Then it was the turn of the Wunny Wuns to pose for the camera. Finally, all the musicians and the entertainers, came together for a group. The officer, now in a tin hat, still sat in the middle.

On the morning of Palm Sunday they played for a church service in the Fusiliers' Hut and then took the lorry to Fouquières to entertain the wounded at the hospital, this time as a military band. Everyone was in a state of some excitement because they had been told to stand to in fighting order, in anticipation of going up the Line on Straggler's Posts. They heard nothing more about this the following morning but at 2 p.m. that afternoon they were inspected in full marching order by

The 'Wunny Wuns' in Pierrot dress with their 'ladies'

Captain Edwardes and found to be 'all satisfactory'. Meanwhile the prints of the photographs arrived and Erskine bought 15 (three of each group) for which he paid 7 francs 50 centimes, to send home to his family and friends.

Orders were made and then countermanded; the 'standing to' never materialised and then, after packing everything up to move on, they were told there had been a change of plans and they were to unpack again. This was around the time of the German Offensive in Picardy which was taking place to the south-west. Erskine noted,

> 'Very critical..........big things on..........French paper says German losses estimated at 150,000 men.'

The German Offensive nearly reached Amiens. Their losses (with hindsight) were actually more like 250,000, the British 164,000 and the French 77,000.

The band continued to practise, playing outdoors when the weather was fine. On Easter Saturday they had to suspend their military band practice while a funeral was held and in the afternoon everyone was on fatigue, from 2 p.m. to 7 p.m., with only a short break

The 11th Divisional Band and the 'Wunny Wuns'

for tea. Their task was to construct an earth embankment to protect a cellar at the Headquarters' château and the fact that it was pouring with rain while they were doing it did not help.

"The Dear Old Deep Bassoon in Action"

The band in action

They had a chance to dry out their clothes on the Sunday but on Easter Monday, just as they were starting their string rehearsal, the call came to do more work on the embankment. The following day, and not before time, Erskine was issued with a new cap. He wrote 'Old one very greasy.'

For the next ten days or so there was little enemy activity and life was a mix of Sunday church service, Pierrots' concert party and playing for the silent movies. One day they entertained the wounded and the doctors and nurses at the 1st Casualty Clearing Station.

Then on 9 April, the order came again to 'stand to' for the Straggler's Post job, which entailed much packing up of equipment. All the spare baggage and heavier instruments were sent to Bruay by lorry, he notes, 'only got one blanket each now.' Throughout the following day there was 'great artillery activity', which tailed off towards the evening - a point noted both by Erskine and the War Diary.

A few days earlier there had been a very heavy gas bombardment over the battery area and the Division's diary reports that some men had been wearing their respirators with the face pieces turned down, a practice that was strictly forbidden.

To nobody's great surprise no more was heard of the Stragglers' Post job. There were always false alarms. On 12 April, both Bruay and Béthune were heavily bombed. The weather was fine and Erskine wrote of his strolls in the surrounding countryside,

'Fine view around here...never think you were so near the war Front.'

Then suddenly, on 13 April, they received hurried orders to leave their billet in Verquin and after another 7 a.m. roll call got ready to leave. They packed up again and were waiting in full marching order when they heard that the job they were supposed to do had been 'washed out': it was yet another false alarm! Later they learnt that they had been going to guard an estaminet in a nearby town where the civilians had already left.

The next day they prepared to play for a Sunday service in the Church Army hut but nobody turned up so that, too, was 'washed out', and they had the day off instead. That night the bandsmen were lying in their beds listening to a 'very busy' battery nearby when the order came 'to shift in the morning - and do some fatigue as well'. It looked as if they really would be leaving.

Bracquemont

*J*T was just getting light when reveille was sounded at 5 a.m. on 15 April. The 11th Division was finally on the move - and had the men but known it, their next destination was to be their home for the best part of the summer. Erskine's diary read,

> 'Travelled by lorry to M......... have previously picked up picks and shovels at L. B.....'

It is not clear why he was censoring his diary - he usually wrote the names of places in full; the L B may have stood for a village called Labourse while the M stood for Mazingarbe. It was at 'M' where the bandsmen and the Pierrots dug a small trench for cable laying purposes near a coal mine. When they completed their fatigue they marched to Bracquemont, a mile south of Noeux-les-Mines, where the DHQ had already taken up residence earlier in the day. They were housed in a 'decent billet', a long wooden hut that held about a hundred men. Erskine wrote,

> 'This hut reminds me of the huts in the camp at Brocton. This is the locality I was in last Christmas so I know the ground well.'

A day or so after they reached Bracquemont the rest of their baggage arrived from the dump at Bruay and Erskine was able to 'have a more comfortable kip with an extra blanket.' There were plenty of fatigues for them to do. One morning, in the middle of a hailstorm, they had to pull down four corrugated iron shanties which had been used as dumps. That night they resumed their roles as musicians and entertained the Signals officers, Erskine playing second fiddle. To their dismay they were not provided with supper.

On Sunday 21 April, after playing for a small church service, the strings gave their first outdoor concert, sitting on a bandstand. Erskine had written a poster advertising the event but few turned out to listen. Later he went for a walk to Hersin, a nearby village, with Kirkham his trombone pal.

Noeux - les - Mines was badly bombed

He noted;

'the country was lovely but the effect is spoiled by a distant view of shells near the Line.'

The oompah - oompah section

The enemy action continued the next day (pay day) 'some of it landing quite close.' It was 'C' Mess's turn to be entertained that night and this time there was more than enough to eat, so someone must have taken the hint.

Military band practice continued, as did the orchestral work. 'The Flying Dutchman' was one of the pieces in their repertoire and Erskine found it 'rather stiff'. One evening the band played for the cinema at the YM in Noeux, where to his surprise he bumped into Commander and Savage, his pals from Brocton. That night he wrote in his diary, 'We've got Givenchy back once more.'

The weather was much warmer now and so he handed in his woollen gloves and heavy leather Army-issue jerkin. Now that he had some new reeds for his oboe Erskine was getting back into his old form. The band used one end of their large hut for practice and rehearsals but it was also home for some other Headquarters men.

The band of the 1st Division visited Bracquemont towards the end of April and Erskine went along to hear it. About this time there was some talk of the Yorkshire Regiment starting a band of its own and although Erskine was interviewed as a possible oboe player he heard no more about it.

The 11th Divisional Band and the 'Wunny Wuns' now had a new officer in charge but the routine continued much the same. Sundays were always busy with a morning service with 'full strings' and, if the weather was fine, a concert in the afternoon. On the last Sunday of April Erskine wrote,

> 'Played a swagger programme of music in the bandstand to admiring crowd - mostly bandsmen of battalion bands.'

The next day he reported,

> 'The number of bandsmen sick is a matter of anxiety...unable to play out this afternoon owing to it. I've got a faint touch of it...high temperature.'

He ended the month with a reference to that day's fatigue,

'Unloading lorries of clean underclothing...bales of 80lbs each...not got the knack of handling them.'   (Sometimes a man would get back his own clean underwear, mostly he did not.)

The War Diary for April ends with the casualty figures - 3 officers and 66 men killed and 55 officers and 1,635 men wounded. It summarises the month, 'Hostile artillery during the month very slight on trenches and confined generally to back areas and battery positions. Many affected by gas.'

May began with a playing out job, travelling by lorry to Hersin-Coupigny which was not very far from the billet. The weather was fine and the men of the Manchesters, encamped in the village, thoroughly enjoyed the military band. In the evening, this time transformed into an orchestra, they played light music in the 34th Brigade HQ Mess in nearby Noeux-les-Mines 'which went off just as well'.

A few days before the Divisional Theatre re-opened Erskine was busy writing posters to announce the date. The 'theatre' was actually a wooden hut, conveniently close to the billet, and some of the band had been busy digging an orchestra pit, using the excavated earth to form a raised area at the rear of the hall so that people at the back could see.

The War Diary notes on 3 May that 'HV guns shelled Noeux and Bracquemont' while Erskine wrote,

'Fritz shelling all morning...set (coal) mine alight...blew up gasometer.'

That evening the strings played for the 'Wunny Wuns' who were making their first appearance in the theatre. Erskine, on second fiddle, admired the new venue but, sitting in the ingenious little orchestra pit that had been dug out of the ground, found space to move his bow 'somewhat limited'.

There was always some event or other where their music was required. They sometimes travelled to Hersin to entertain the Lincolns, another of the 11th Division's infantry regiments. Whenever they were free they played for the cinema, though sometimes they sat behind a blanket 'screen' which meant they couldn't see the film. Erskine did not explain how they knew when it was time to play.

On 8 May the band took the lorry to Mazingarbe where the Staffords were holding their sports. This was technically still his 'mob' as his transfer to the Labour Corps hadn't yet come through. It

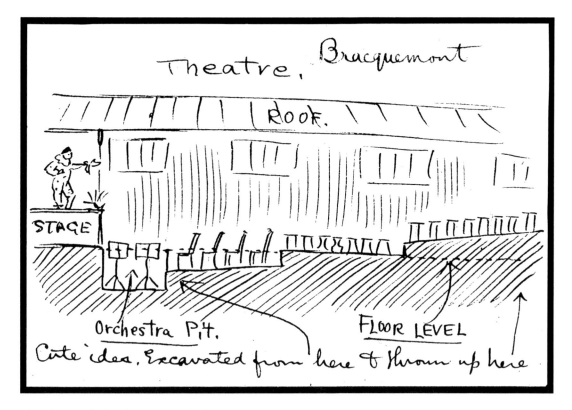

A view of the improved theatre

was a glorious day and they joined in the fun by taking part in the band race, playing a tune as they ran - which was easier for some than others.

The BASS in the Band Race. at Sports

(This Was Actually Done) Muzingarbe

Making music on the move

The next day there was renewed excitement; once more everybody was ordered to stand by, ready to go near the Line on Straggler's Post duty, but just like the last time it proved to be a false alarm.

Life went on at Bracquemont. One day Erskine visited the clothing stores to replace some of his uniform, but there was nothing in stock; then he tried to get a much-needed bath, but again he was unsuccessful. There was nothing for it; he would have to wait a little longer.

May 15 was something of a landmark in Erskine's military career for this was when he officially transferred from the South Staffordshire Regiment to the Labour Corps and was posted to 213 Company. This meant that he would no longer wear the Staffordshire Knot in the front of his cap; instead he would wear a badge which was the same as the Royal coat of arms. Despite the move it made little difference to his daily round.

Erskine drew the CO on the back of an envelope

O/C South Staffs 7th Pct.

The C.O Enjoys the Band

Sports at Mazingarbe.

Bullets and Bandsmen

It was quite a hectic day; in the morning, after practising with the band for a full three hours, he was ordered to paint a picture of a Welsh railway station as a scene for the Pierrots' concert party. It was already Wednesday and it had to be finished by Friday. May 15 was a busy day for Fritz as well because he spent some time lobbing shells into the area. Erskine noted tersely, 'casualties'. One of the shells landed behind the theatre during the show. The War Diary that day reports that high velocity guns had shelled Bracquemont, that balloons were up on both sides and hostile aircraft were active. The enemy was undoubtedly getting closer and the DHQ was making emergency arrangements in case they had to withdraw.

Erskine wrote,

> 'Fritz has got a new gag...strafes us with high velocity gun from 5 a.m. to 8 a.m ...pretty near us, too.'

The War Diary confirms this, 'Bracquemont shelled early in the morning.' But in addition, 'Attack on enemy trenches successful, slight casualties,' so Fritz was not having it all his own way. Nonetheless Béthune was undeniably suffering a massive bombardment for on 19 May Erskine noted that the town was burning, and the following day, again, 'Béthune and another place burning.'

Shortly after Whit Monday, when Erskine was enjoying a siesta, the Military Police called upon him to do some artistic work for them - painting, in white, their 'GR' badge on eight tin helmets. He went over to the Police Lines to carry out the job 'which gave great satisfaction' and the next day after doing a few more helmets he began to paint the badge on some sword hilts when suddenly the job was cancelled, 'much against the inclination of the AMP' (sic).

The following day he handed in his pay book because from now on he would be paid as a member of 213 Employment Company. Some days later he started wearing the new 'Government' cap badge, producing much comment from some of his pals when the band next played for the Staffords. By the end of the week he had finished painting the helmets and he wasn't sorry either; it hurt his eyes and kept him away from his band practice.

Towards the end of May the Taubes were regular nightly visitors, droning overhead and keeping everyone awake. The news from the Front was not good and on 29 May the War Diary records that the Germans had been dropping pamphlets about an offensive on the Aisne. On 31 May Erskine noted,

> 'Fritz making big advance near Soissons, over the Rivers Aisne and Vesle....seems to be going strong.'

That night the Pierrots played, as usual, to a full house and among the audience was the Divisional General. The war news was as bad, the following day, 1 June,

AT THE "M.M.P'S".
Painting badge on Tin Hats.
at Bracquement

A paint job for the Military Police

'Germans reported making further progress...between Rheims and Soissons. Not at all good news.'

But at least there were no visits from the Taubes that night.

One of Erskine's less enjoyable fatigues was floor scrubbing, particularly at 6 a.m. After the floors were washed and breakfast was over he finished painting the scenery. In the afternoon he played his oboe in Hersin Square, for the benefit of the locals. Finding a vehicle to take them on these trips was not always easy and when they finally commandeered one that afternoon it took them all round the houses to get to their destination. In the evening he swapped his oboe for the violin and played at the camp cinema for the film 'Bitter Truth'. Afterwards he went for a stroll and then noted in his diary,

'New orders: not allowed beyond the billeting area without a pass.'

Things were certainly tightening up.

On 8 June the Sherwood Foresters raided the enemy lines, inflicting casualties. Their own losses were low - one officer killed, three officers and eleven men wounded, one officer and a man missing. The band were now quite used to Fritz's presence when they were performing. Occasionally the theatre lights went out during a performance but they usually carried on when there was a raid. However, there were some close shaves. On 10 June Erskine wrote,

'Fritz landed a few shells near our billet as we set off for Hersin to play in the Square...one right in our officer's billet. Fortunately he was out.'

The next day Erskine noted that Fritz had made some advances on the Somme 'with great losses'. Alongside this he made a note that he had a new pair of trousers, which did not fit properly and had to be altered at a cost of Fr. 1.50.

Sailly Labourse was the inspiration for Scene I

The enemy meanwhile was getting bolder. On 16 June he noted,

> 'Fritz very rude this morning. Gave us two doses of the 2 inch variety, not far away. Fragments descended over a huge radius. We were at church service during second spasm...we stuck it.'

The Fun Merchants at R.E. Sports. HERSIN. P.de.C.

Observe Camouflaged body of the "Motor"

The R.E Sports

In spite of the morning's activity they all went to play that afternoon at the Royal Engineers' Sports at Hersin, where they spotted ten of Fritz's balloons in the sky.

The following day was extremely hot and as there was no official church service he carried on with the scenery. The work was carried out in an airy wooden hut with a tarred paper roof ('my scenic studio') and from time to time people would wander in and watch him at work. That night there was 'great aerial activity from Fritz' who dropped five bombs close by, leaving huge great holes in the ground. Erskine slept in the dugout with the other bandsmen. He wrote,

> 'No one killed during night or even injured.'

They slept there again the following night but Fritz did not turn up so after that they returned to their billet.

While Erskine was busy with the scenery the Pierrots were busy rehearsing because their new show, The Five Knights, was due to open in only two days' time. On 3 July they held their first full dress rehearsal. The next day a party of Royal Engineers fixed up the 'limes' (lights) in the roof of the theatre and that night, even though the wings were not quite ready, they staged the final full dress rehearsal, with 'buckshee' admission to the hall. Now fully rehearsed, the revue finally opened to a full house and The Five Knights went with a swing. When the Pierrots had taken their final curtain call the Band Master, the pianist, Jones the first violin, the man who worked the

One of the Five Knights

limelights and Erskine the scene painter were presented to the audience and each had his own ovation.

After that first performance word soon spread and plenty of seats were sold in advance. To publicise it further Erskine painted a large poster showing a knight in armour, an eye-catching caricature with a larger-than-life head. For the first week of the show there had been hardly any enemy activity. The War Diary notes that it was 'abnormally quiet.' But on 15 July Fritz was back in the air though the revue went ahead as usual.

On the last night of the show, 17 July, it was so hot that the bandsmen played in their shirt sleeves. Erskine noted how unusual this was, 'Strange to see us with coats off'. The pianist for some reason did not play that night, so Mr Marshall, their CO, played instead - and he was wearing full evening dress.

The War Diary for that day records, 'Successful raid on trenches, most of the casualties caused by following their barrage too closely'. Two days later it reads, 'Bombardment of enemy trenches'. Was the course of the war about to change?

A Battlefield Tour

*L*IFE at Bracquemont was rarely dull; they never knew where they would be playing next. They had some most unusual venues: the latest was 'a grand boxing competition at Hersin-Coupigny in fine wooded grounds, a capitally arranged affair'. Erskine, not normally a boxing fan, found it 'good sport' but bemoaned the fact that tea was not provided.

The war news filtering through to them was of a big capture by the French of 17,000 prisoners, as well as many guns, which Erskine amended the following day to '20,000 prisoners and 400-odd guns.' The news from home was not so good because he received a letter from his brother Frank to say that little Ralph, his nephew, had died of pneumonia.

Good news from home always raised morale and the men were eager for the mail to arrive. Some of Erskine's sketches showed the men reading their mail or writing their replies. Their other occupations in such spare time as they had seemed to be taking naps, playing cards and - the latest craze - learning French, no doubt the better to chat to the girls.

One night, towards the end of July, when the bandsmen were in the dugout, Fritz dropped a massive bomb close by and Erskine noted 'some were killed'. He did not say whether they were Service personnel or civilians, though it was probably the latter. Strangely there was no reference to the incident in the War Diary which two days earlier had reported, 'Seventh South Staffs patrol took the initiative and on coming across an enemy party of about 28 inflicted several casualties'.

Many thousands of men from the Colonies such as the ANZACs (Australian and New Zealand Army Corps) and the Canadians were playing a vital part in the fight against the Boche. Erskine sketched a soldier of the Australian Tunnelling Company wearing the distinctive headgear, turned up at the side. The Aussies even had their own cinema where Erskine saw a film called 'The Darling of Paris,' of which he remarked in his diary that it was a 'Good story'.

Australian
Tunneling
Company

Orders

Bracquemont

The Aussies

On 29 July the Pierrots took The Five Knights on tour, and the bandsmen went too. They all crowded into the lorry to travel west to Pernes, a village on the other side of Bruay. There they presented the revue for the benefit of the 4th Canadian Casualty Clearing Station, playing to a full house in a wooden theatre, with nurses and doctors in the front row of the stalls. That night they all slept in a huge marquee, to be woken by reveille at 6.30 a.m. ready for an early breakfast of boiled egg and fried bacon.

As well as accompanying the revue the band gave a military concert while they were there, playing some of the ten new marches they had recently added to their repertoire. The marquee, it turned out, had been only a temporary billet and on the second day at Pernes they moved all their things into a 'sort of temporary hospital hut', sleeping that night more comfortably on stretchers propped on wooden trestles.

The weather was fine and one day Erskine watched the swimmers in the open air bath, splashing about and having fun. It wasn't every day that they could go for a swim. Another time he listened to the 52nd Divisional Band as they played in the village square. The band was a Scots outfit, the bandsmen wearing Tam o' Shanter headgear bearing a badge with the thistle and St Andrew's flag.

On 1 August they packed up and set off on the next leg of their tour, this time back to Bruay where they showed The Five Knights in a tiny hall. Erskine noted, 'Poor rations here.' Their billet was in a brewery; they had hardly any sleep, thanks to the presence of Fritz in the air. There was very little to eat the following morning, just hard tack biscuits and the inevitable bully beef, and soon afterwards they left by lorry to perform at another Headquarters, this one some distance away at

A Canadian medic at Pernes

The 52nd Divisional Band - 'a Scots outfit'

Ferfay, back in the direction of Pernes. Then they returned, in a roundabout way, to their familiar quarters at Bracquemont. The War Diary notes 'Patrol entered enemy Front Line and captured two prisoners of the 10th Ersatz (Reinforcement) Division and then interrogated them.'

August 4 was a date that everyone remembered for it was the anniversary of the outbreak of war, four long years ago. To mark the occasion a special church service was held that evening at the DHQ, with the full orchestra providing suitably solemn music. The sermon was given by the Bishop of Khartoum, who had preached to them last year. They were not to know that in less than three weeks they would be leaving Bracquemont - to become part of the Great Advance to Victory.

Meanwhile they settled down as if they had never been away. The Five Knights revue was to be replaced by a new Pierrot show so it was back into the familiar black and white costumes with pompoms and ruff. The 'Wunny Wuns' needed some advertising signs and naturally Erskine was roped in to paint them. This meant getting another pass and going to the shop in Petit Sain to buy paints and varnish. It took him about a week to paint the canvas yellow, write the lettering and coat it with varnish.

The weather was exceptionally hot and there was dust everywhere. The orchestra played in their shirt sleeves in the evenings for the cinema. The candles they used to help them see the music would gradually bend - 'very despondent and curly'. One evening Erskine leant a hand with the projector, helping Firth turn his Gaumont machine, which was 'jolly hot work'.

One morning early in August Erskine was on floor scrubbing fatigue in the nearby château but he was quite cheered up by the war news, which was good. On 9 August he wrote,

> 'We are doing well on the Somme. Great Advance.'

The War Diary entry that day reads, 'Fifty believed to be killed and others wounded during a raid by us'. But the next day it notes that, 'Enemy aircraft very active bombing the back areas...about 75 bombs dropped in and near Bracquemont.' This tallies with Erskine's diary in which he wrote,

> 'Fritz came over in relays this evening, kept it up till 3.30 a.m. Much
> excitement...some killed and wounded at the Australians' camp during raid.'

Noeux-les-Mines, a kilometre or so to the north was having a bad time. For the next few days there was heavy shelling, both in the morning and the afternoon.

In spite of the enemy activity the band continued their engagements; they played at Houdain for the Royal Artillery Sports and attended a horse show where they played on a bandstand in a 'magnificently appointed sports ground'.

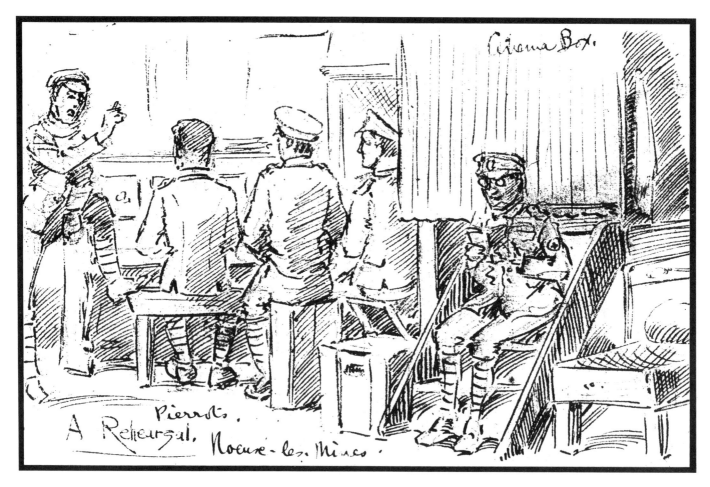

The Pierrots rehearsed their show

A few days later they returned to Houdain to see another concert party, the 1st Army Pierrots called 'Les Rouges et Noirs'. The next day, 18 August, the 'Wunny Wuns' troupe travelled to a nearby Hersin to have their photo taken wearing their Five Knights costumes. A week later the pictures were ready and everyone was ordering copies to send home.

'The Five Knights' company (Erskine is the soldier standing centre)

Friday 23 August was an eventful day. Erskine wrote,

> 'Preparing for a move. Grand packing up all day. I've been helping load lorry
> with laundry stuff, bales of shirts etc. Rather heavy work. War news good.'

The instruments were packed on Saturday. On Sunday, before they left, he wrote,

> 'A lazy day. Nothing on save just helping to load a lorry with wood and forms
> from the theatre. War news still continues good.'

The Allies had renewed their offensive and the Division was on its way.

The War Diary for Monday, 26 August reads, 'Orders received to the effect that the remainder of the Division, less Artillery, was to be ready to move at two hours' notice to north of Arras'. Three days later it reports that the move had taken place as planned and that the DHQ was now established in that dreadfully bomb-scarred town. However the band took the journey in stages and so took twice as long to get there. Their usual mode of transport, a GS lorry, took them in a south-westerly direction to a small village called Mingoval where their billet was a tumble-down barn. The cookhouse was in the middle of a field and Erskine, as Orderly Man during their brief stay, had the task of drawing water from the well. It was still exceptionally warm and most of the men slept under the stars.

On 28 August he wrote,

> 'Holding ourselves in readiness to move. Saw wounded Fritzes at hospital.'

The next night, after a lengthy wait, and wearing their full uniform they took the lorry to Maroeuil, a small village to the north-west of Arras; they tried to get some sleep in their crowded bow hut but

Visé Paris n° 2727
ARRAS. — L'Hôtel de Ville. — The Town-Hall.

Edition Duclos-Grassin

Bomb damaged Arras

were kept awake most of the night by the sound of the shelling.

Incredibly, some of the French countryside had escaped the ravages of war and though they were near the Line they still managed to enjoy the rural atmosphere. Erskine wrote,

> 'Situated right in the country, nothing but huts and little dugouts. Had nice ramble in woods gathering nuts. All very pleasant.'

Bullets and Bandsmen

Two days before they left the village Erskine discovered a dugout that had evidently been occupied by a Sergeant Major. It was furnished with a wire bunk bed and a table, it had a door and was dry and quite comfortable to live in and enjoy a decent night's sleep. While they were at Maroueil two men on Straggler's Post duty discovered a soldier who had lost his way and the next day he was returned to his outfit.

On 1 September they left for Arras by lorry, a distance of about 4 kilometres. Erskine was appalled by the devastation.

> 'Such a sight there. Place terribly strafed. We were billeted in barracks, very ancient buildings. Shelling near by and Fritz overhead. Very bad night.'

For almost three weeks Arras was their base; it was also where many thousands of German prisoners were held in the local civilian prison. Erskine noted,

> 'We have made a big advance and seem to be doing well. I spoke to some of the Fritzes in German...they seem fairly happy.' But there was still plenty of enemy activity, he continued, 'Fritz shells with a long range gun...all go in same place after travelling overhead with a fearsome scream... Fritz strafes the same place, two or three times a day. One landed quite near the barracks.'

The instruments had not yet caught up with the band but there were plenty of jobs for them to do while they waited. Four of the men helped with the prisoners, some directed the traffic. Four others, including Erskine, had to clean and scrub a room for a major at the DHQ. That same evening he went for a walk with his pal Jones round some old fortifications in the town; another day they went to look at some German ammunition dumps.

Time for a different sort of solo

Both Erskine and the DHQ diary recorded one particularly noisy night,

'Shelling from 9 p.m. last night till 8 a.m. this morning. Rare dose of it.
Shocking night's sleep in an unused stable on ground floor of the barracks.'

The official record reads, 'Arras shelled by HV guns in night. Our heavy artillery hit back.' It was the same for the next two nights. Erskine continued,

> 'Very heavy dose of high velocity shelling all night. During the day had a few huge shrapnels overhead. Chunk fell in front of our quarters...(Shifted case of wine for C Mess from one house to another).'

On 9 September their instruments finally arrived, although they were missing the cornets which meant that Jones had to go back to Tincques to fetch them. After an impromptu rehearsal the band played in the ruined square to entertain the Sherwood Foresters, and after tea they played to the South Staffs in a corridor in the Art Gallery. They gave a concert for the Yorks, in the courtyard of a fine old building that had somehow escaped the shelling, and performed at a Hospital run by the Canadians.
Erskine noted,

> 'Very pleasant conditions. Well appreciated. Gave us a great tea afterwards (they call it supper). Did enjoy it. Salmon, sardines, tongue and custard, etc.'

On 13 September The War Diary reports that Major General H. Davies, CB, who commanded the Division, was wounded while making an inspection and evacuated to the Casualty Clearing Station. Meanwhile Erskine noted in his diary,

> 'News of big doings by Yankees down South.'

The Germans had been driven out of the St Mihiel salient, south of Verdun, by the American First Army.

On 19 September the band left Arras to start their tour, travelling 23 kilometres or so back to Tincques where they had been some time before (and where some of their luggage was still dumped). Tincques was some distance from the Line, which meant they should be able to get some sleep, but first they had to find a billet which turned out to be a barn with 'very dilapidated wire beds'.

As part of their tour they played for two open air church services - at Frévillers for the Royal Engineers and at Cambligneul for the Machine Gun Company. Their only other commitment was to play for the Pierrots at the 7th CCS at Ligny, where they later sat down to a 'very swell knife and fork supper in the Sergeants' Mess'.

On 23 September while the band was practising in the cinema the order came to shift. 'Must be a stunt, I think' wrote Erskine. All the spare stuff was hastily packed up and left in the dump and everyone climbed into the lorry which took them to the station at Savvy-Berlette. From there they travelled in railway trucks to Bullecourt on the far side of Arras, towards the Line, then they marched to a village called Croissiles. It was deserted so they slept the night in a trench. The next day Erskine wrote,

'First night I've slept without a roof, some of the shells pretty close.'

The next night they found a dug out on the railway embankment and had just got comfortably settled when the orders came again to shift, so they packed up once more and set off on foot. It was the middle of the night and pouring with rain. After marching 8 kilometres or so they arrived at Chérisy, another deserted village where they 'couldn't find anybody or anything'. Finally, at 3 a.m. a lorry came along and as many as possible climbed in, leaving 13 of the musicians behind to find their way to the next village. But there were compensations: 'Saw grand sunrise to barrage accompaniment.'

On Stragglers' Post,
Sauchy Lestree

Keeping an eye for stragglers who have lost their way

Meanwhile the War Diary notes, '32nd - 34th Infantry Brigade attacked and captured Epinoy and Oisy-le-Verger.' These were two villages to the east, near Cambrai, and not so very far from where they were. Erskine had little idea of where they were heading but it turned out to be Cagnicourt, which was also in the direction of Cambrai. He wrote,

'Don't know what we are doing.
Supposed to be attached to the C.C.'

That night they slept in a cellar in the ruins of a house. The following day, Saturday 28 September, they all marched on to Buissy, which was up the Line a bit and where the DHQ was now based. There was a POW cage at Buissy and the next day Erskine guarded some of the men while they were on a digging fatigue, speaking some German to the Fritz corporal.

They moved on again, marching up towards the Line and over the Nord Canal where they had a narrow escape from the bullets and the shelling. Erskine was put on Straggler's Post which he thought 'quite an easy job' with three of the other bandsmen. He noted that, 'We got one straggler'. Their billet was a cellar in another ruined house, near the village of Sauchy-Lestrée. A man called Day was the cook and as he was the oldest soldier in the group he was temporarily in charge.

> 'Get decent meals, though the rations small, and have them quite respectably in
> the cellar with a salvaged table and form from Fritz's vacated billets.'

Their instruments were still at Tincques and they had no idea when they would catch up with them. But at least the war news was good.

The Great Advance

*I*T could be very lonely during the night watch - 'We do two hours on and four off' - but there was usually plenty of action, in the direction of the Line where guns flashed all the time. Erskine wrote,

> 'It's a rare experience to be here, so close to the Lines. Fritz shells the main Cambrai Road with big black beauties that scream over our heads.'

October was to be another month when the band and the Pierrots were swept along in the wake of the Great Advance. Unlike the men of the infantry brigades they were not exposed to any great degree of danger but they still had their part to play. Of the Dorsets Erskine noted, 'they have taken a difficult position, a railway embankment.'

Scraps of news reached them about other countries at war, that Bulgaria had unconditionally surrendered and Turkey had turned it in; later they learned that this referred to the 8th Turkish Army and not the actual country. On 7 October Erskine wrote,

> 'Hear Germany wants armistice to consider Wilson's peace terms.'

One of Erskine's jobs was fetching the rations from DHQ Stores at Buissy; another was getting the water from Sauchy - Lestrée, the village near their billet, preferably when there was a lull in the shelling. Early one morning when he was on watch from 4 a.m. to 6 a.m. Fritz was busy with his planes - 'dropping a lot all round, but fortunately not on us'. He watched the dawn, thankful that it would soon be daylight when the aerial bombing would stop.

Night shelling

Bullets and Bandsmen

The hours dragged slowly by whenever he was on duty at night; he was always glad when his relief turned up when he would wrap himself in his blanket and try to get some sleep despite the noise of the artillery. The War Diary entry for 6 October reads, 'Occupied Abancourt Station (north of Cambrai),' but two days later it says, 'Enemy got it back.' However they did not have it long for the next day Erskine wrote in his diary that they had heard that Cambrai and 'three kilometres beyond' was back in the hands of the Allies. He wrote,

> 'Fritz retreating in this sector and is well away from here. Think we shall be going further up soon, according to the reports we get.'

The reports turned out to be true and on 10 October they packed up and left Sauchy-Lestrée, making their way on foot and by lorry to Bantigny, another ruined village close to Abancourt where the railway station had so recently changed hands.

They were now close to Cambrai. Erskine wrote,

> 'Landed in a very hot quarter, near our guns, incessant firing, lot of shelling....narrow escape while on guard... very hot.' (He never explained what happened.)

At Bantigny they found another billet that had been vacated by Fritz - 'decent cellar with civvy beds and very comfortable'. It had a stove on which they cooked their rations and an oil lamp for light. Outside it was nowhere near as pleasant. He wrote,

> 'This is a very rotten and unhealthy locality...defunct Fritzes lying near our billet.'

IN CELLAR COOL.

BISCUITS.

A Cosy Corner in a Warm Spot. BANTIGNY.

Bantigny - a rather hot spot

On 12 October he saw column after column of Canadian soldiers passing through the village on the way to the Front and the very next day they received orders to leave and hand over the post - to the Canadians. Erskine added in his diary: 'along with boiled spuds and greens.'

Bullets and Bandsmen

Their destination this time was Baralle, the other side of Sauchy-Lestrée, where they had been quite recently; now they were back with the DHQ, or at least part of it because it had recently split into three separate echelons. Instead of a cellar their billet this time was a 'decent house, though rather bashed about'. It had been fitted with little cubicles, each containing two wire beds, one above the other; they were not surprised to learn that the previous occupants had been Germans.

After the constant artillery noise where they had been before they had a really peaceful night and the following day marched some distance to Inchy-en-Artois where they enjoyed the rare luxury of a hot bath and a change of underclothes. There was another rumour on 15 October, this time that there would be a 90-hour armistice for Fritz to evacuate to Germany. But it was indeed only a rumour. Erskine wrote,

'We are going to fight. Our stern resolve...pity, thought peace was at hand.'

That day he had been on fatigue filling sandbags to protect a building at the HQ. People had been coming and going on leave of late and one of his pals, Simpson, had to return to his ambulance which meant they were short of men for fatigues. Erskine was given yet another floor scrubbing job because they had to clean up a room for the GSO 2 which was full of debris from the shelling. The instruments finally appeared at 4 p.m. on 17 October, arriving by lorry from Tincques. There was a good chance that they might actually be using them soon but until then the fatigues continued. The latest one was transporting a load of dirty linen by lorry back to Arras 'travelling through the stricken land.' When they arrived they loaded more washing into lorries and took it on to Cambrai, finally returning to Bantigny at 3.30 a.m. the following morning.

The next day they had a late start to compensate for their lack of sleep and then the band all travelled to Sailly, where they entertained the men of the 34th Brigade HQ. They stayed there a couple of nights, billeted in a ground floor room. Afterwards their instruments were packed up and sent away, this time to the dump at nearby Cambrai. The men packed up as well and set off by foot

...and how it feels

and by lorry to Naves, another small village, about 6 kilometres from Cambrai, where they stayed for over a week.

The main fatigue of note at Naves was burying gas shells that had been left behind on a partially blown-up dump. First they had to dig holes some eight feet deep and then, taking the greatest care, the shells had to be stacked at the bottom before they were covered over. Erskine wrote,

Laundry fatigue - how it looks.......

BURYING GAS SHELLS.

(A dangerous one
with detonator
exposed)

NAVES,

Burying the dangerous gas shells

'Only buried the dangerous shells...some had to be handled carefully, being detonated.'

After the job was completed it was pay day and Erskine was re-paid most of his loans. For a day or two there was very little to do and as their billet was quite homely 'other chaps come to visit us'. A batch of papers arrived from Blighty - miraculously they always caught up with them, even when they were on the move - and were eagerly devoured for news. Erskine wrote,

'Fritz's answer to Wilson is vague and unsatisfactory. No signs of peace as yet. Belgian coast cleared of the enemy, which is a great thing...strange being here and doing so little.'

A week or so after the instruments went back to Cambrai they suddenly returned on 26 October - for a playing job which never materialised. Instead Erskine found himself on fatigue, shifting a load of manure and 'other rubbish and filth.' The following morning, in what remained of someone's back garden, the new bandmaster, Sergeant McMahon conducted a small band rehearsal and for the next few days they resumed their playing out jobs, usually at the village crossroads.

One evening some of his chums, always resourceful, decided to make a bread pudding but Erskine felt off colour and just couldn't face it. The following day his appetite had returned ('cleared up my share of the duff'). That afternoon they travelled 7 kilometres in the direction of the Line to a Brigade HQ at Villers-en-Cauchies, where they played at the cross roads to a group of troops. The day after that they played even nearer the Line; this was Haspres where they saw the sad sight of streams of refugees, passing through the village with all that remained of their possessions. The month ended with yet more rumours. One was that U-boats had been seen returning with white flags flying, another that Turkey was signing an armistice. It looked as if peace was really on the way.

There was just one more playing job while they were at Naves and that was entertaining officers of the Machine Gun Corps on the landing of the stairs of their mess ('a very noisy performance') and the next morning the band packed up their instruments. Howarth, who played the fiddle, returned off leave but Erskine's hopes of a pass were fading - 'it's very distant now' he wrote.
The musicians were now under the orders of the Assistant Provost Marshal (of the Military Police) and their duty was to guard the prisoners' cages. On Sunday 3 November, they took the lorry to Verchain almost due south of the city of Valenciennes. Erskine wrote,

'Pierrots on this 'do' with us. I'm in the party for the rear cage. Fetched back three Fritz prisoners.'

Guarding the war cage

The cage in question was at Quérénaing 5 kilometres ahead and so, briefly, was the DHQ. Now that Fritz was retiring so rapidly the cages were filling up. He wrote,

> 'Good bunch of prisoners. Did turn of guard. Spoke a lot to Fritzes...they were pleased to speak to someone.'

The War Diary adds on 3 November, 'Ascertained the enemy was withdrawing opposite our front. No opposition.'

After one night they were off again, via Artres, for Préseau to join up with the DHQ. They seemed to be moving every other day. The advance was going strong but their progress was held up that

On traffic control at Artres

day by heavy enemy machine gun fire. While they were at Préseau Erskine and another bandsman were sent back to Artres to undertake traffic control duty, standing in the rain for three hours at a stretch, followed by six hours off, round the clock. Erskine wrote,

> 'Feet getting bad. Boots rather thin. Overcoat and ground sheet on. Plenty to do when long strings of traffic are passing in contrary directions. Nothing doing during the night, very little traffic.'

By 7 November the DHQ had reached Curgies; they were moving every few days in a north-easterly direction in the wake of the battle. The War Diary reads, 'Opposition very slight and casualties very few. Orders issued for 32nd and 33rd Infantry Brigade to continue the advance tomorrow morning, the railway east of Aulnois the objective'. That day Erskine wrote,

> 'On the traffic regulating job again, rained all day. Miserable. Had the usual headache. Off my feed. Water gets in boots.' (But things were not all bad.) 'Peace talk rumours...seems as if it's coming off. Good.'

The next day he wrote, 'Expect the good news every hour.' Meanwhile they had to catch up with the DHQ which was on the move again. They set off at around 2 p.m. marching to Curgies along dismal muddy roads. 'Saw French refugees. Pitiable plight.' There were many people worse off than he.

On 9 November everything was on the move. The advance, they heard, was going strong and they were part of it, marching along the busy, traffic-lined roads from Curgies to Roisin and then to Autreppe. Erskine was cold and muddy but the war news was so good that he allowed himself to think about home. Perhaps he would soon be going back to Blighty - for good.

HOW
IT
LOOKS.

Obelisk Commemorating
a War (1709)

MALPLAQUET,
Day before Armistice

CUTTING OFF CORNERS, VIA THE FIELDS.
SOME MUD. BEAUCOUP FATIGUE.

The advance - how it looks....

It had been hard getting enough rations while they were on the move and all they had to keep them going was 'makeshift grub'. They were once again in Belgium; it seemed a long time since they were there before, further north, during the Third Battle of Ypres.

......and how it feels

The next morning,10 November, the traffic men, about 50 in all, had a hurried breakfast before marching the 18 kilometres to Aulnois where once again the DHQ had sprinted ahead and set up another temporary base to conduct operations. Erskine noted that every time they came to cross roads they had been blown up by mines so that they had to march across the fields. These were even muddier than the roads and were littered with ammunition boxes and empty shell cases.

On arrival at Aulnois they found a billet in a 'fine empty house' which somehow had escaped the shelling. To his surprise, in spite of the dreadful weather, Erskine was feeling in remarkably good health. 'Rumours of peace tomorrow,' he wrote. And the rumours were true. The war was finally over. He wrote,

> 'On the stroke of 11 o'clock on the 11th month, the 11th Divisional Band played National airs in front of the château. Cessation of hostilities for Armistice..Fritz accepts our terms. Marched through village. Played programme in street this afternoon. Wet. On Band work now.'

The entry in the War Diary for 11 November reads, 'Orders received and issued that hostilities will cease at 1100 hrs. Brigades to stand fast on Line when reached and report disposition to DHQ. Weather fine. (Odd that the weather record was so different.) 'Issued orders for maintenance of roads in brigade areas.' Work had to go on even though the war had ended. The following day Erskine still could not believe it. He wrote,

> 'Gradually getting used to the new conditions of Peace. Lovely not to be in fear of enemy shelling. Pierrot corporals off to Cambrai to fetch all baggage. Entertainment going to be started. Nice not to fear aerial visitors although lovely moon tonight.'

That afternoon they played military music in the centre of the village and a day or so later entertained the wounded and the staff at the ambulance station where Simpson had been working. 14 November was a free day so some of them bandsmen went for a stroll. Though it was cold the weather was fine so Erskine and his friends went to inspect the nearby Malplaquet monument.

Two great dates in November 1918

During their time at Aulnois they played at the 33rd Field Ambulance football match at Goegnies. Erskine was glad to get back to the billet because he was felt so unwell (and he was not the only one in the band to feel that way). Simpson took his temperature and found it to be 101 degrees, which was 'rather high'. Seven men slept in one small room so it was not surprising that they caught one another's infections, in this case believed to be 'flu.

On 15 November the War Diary notes that a 'Party of all ranks attended a parade at Mons for the official entry of the Army Command into the town'. Erskine wrote,

> 'There was a big demonstration at Mons. Wish we had been there with our band.'

Two days later, in spite of their influenza, they played at Mass in the local church. Because the weather was cold and so many of the band were unwell they were excused their next job, an outside concert for the Royal Artillery. There was no excuse the following day because they had an indoor engagement, playing for the Royal Engineers in the hall of the château. The following night the audience were wearing some 'strange uniforms'; they turned out to be repatriated prisoners of war from Germany.

Some of the bandsmen were going on leave and some of them were returning but the ever-present topic was demobilisation - 'much query about who is going first and who isn't'. Erskine was expecting some leave fairly soon but on 23 November there were rumours of yet another move. For the next few days they gave concerts, played for the silent movies and accompanied the concert party. George Robey was at the height of his popularity and the Pierrots' comedian did a passable imitation; the act went down well with the audience when 'The Prime Minister of Mirth' appeared in front of the footlights, with huge painted-on eyebrows and tiny hat.

A few days before the end of the month they packed up for their final move, this time west to Denain, where the DHQ was now installed. This was to be the centre for all the Division's

"CEASE THIS UNSEEMLY LEVITY."

Our Comedian.

George Robey, a popular character to imitate

educational and recreational training. The bandsmen and the Pierrots arrived in the dark after a 30-mile lorry ride (Erskine was already thinking in Imperial measures); the roads on the way had been very bad and the Royal Engineers had hurriedly replaced broken bridges with wooden ones.

The theatre where the 'Wunny Wuns' were to appear was quite magnificent, an opera house with room for 50 musicians in the orchestra pit. Erskine wrote,

'Can't understand this town
having such a grand place. Fritz
doesn't seem to have behaved so
badly here, according to
civilians' yarns.'

The billet in Denain was quite good, as billets go, this time in a private house with his friend Jones. Meanwhile the Pierrots - and the orchestra - were busy rehearsing for the new show.

The War Diary records that H.M. The King visited Condé, just north of Valenciennes on 5 December where he had lunch and received the G.O.C.

December 6 was a red letter day in Erskine's diary for he was going on leave at last. He caught a lorry loaded with coal to Valenciennes, travelling in another to the railhead at Raismes. There he found the Reception Camp where he drew Fr. 200 from the Disbursing Officer, had some tea and retired in the big rest billet.

Erskine got up at 3.30 the next morning and ate 'a modest breakfast of bread, bacon and tea', then it was off in the dark to the station where he waited for the train to the coast, which finally arrived at midday, already full of soldiers who had got on at Valenciennes.

It was a full 24 hours before he got to Boulogne, feeling 'very fed up...no grub'. However after marching to a billet near the quay he was given a good hot dinner and had a much needed wash before making his way along the cobbled streets to catch the ferry. After long delays the 'Victoria,' loaded as ever with servicemen, finally berthed at Folkestone Harbour, by which time it was dusk. Erskine caught the train to London, arriving at Victoria by 7.25 p.m. and then, suddenly, he was home. He wrote,

> 'It's a treat to be in the land of comfort and civilisation once more. Overjoyed with the prospect of not returning to France. Strange to observe roads like billiard tables.'

The potholes and craters, the mud and the duckboards would be soon be only a memory. On New Year's Eve he wrote the last words in his diary,

> 'Boy Scouts sounded All Clear tonight - but we didn't hear it.'

Not only was Little Jim finished for the day, Erskine was demobbed while he was in England

Epilogue

ERSKINE was demobilised on 2 February 1919 and duly issued with the British War and Victory medals. He resumed his career as a technical illustrator and married Violet Smith in April 1924, two days before her 22nd birthday. Three month's later Erskine's father died and he started his own sign writing business in the house he had bought in Tooting a few streets away. Sadly the 21 years age difference between Erskine and his wife proved too much and their marriage broke up during the Second World War. His daughter, Daphne Jones, found his diaries and sketch book among his effects when he died in London in 1951, a month before his 70th birthday.

Compared to the men who fought in the trenches Erskine had an easy war, but he saw some terrible sights and for much of his time on the Western Front he endured heavy bombardment. He was deeply affected by his experiences. Throughout her childhood, Daphne never heard him mention the war and the only sign that he had ever been a soldier was the tin hat, bearing the Staffordshire knot which hung on his workshop wall.